Leckie✕Leckie
Scotland's leading educational publishers

CfE Higher
GEOGRAPHY
SUCCESS GUIDE

CfE Higher GEOGRAPHY SUCCESS GUIDE

Laura Greig • Samantha Peck
Akiko Tomitaka

001/19062015

10 9 8 7 6 5 4 3 2

ISBN 9780007554447

Published by
Leckie & Leckie Ltd
An imprint of HarperCollins*Publishers*
Westerhill Road, Bishopbriggs, Glasgow, G64 2QT
T: 0844 576 8126   F: 0844 576 8131
leckieandleckie@harpercollins.co.uk
www.leckieandleckie.co.uk

Publisher: Katherine Wilkinson
Project manager: Craig Balfour

Special thanks to
Louise Robb (copy edit and proofread)
QBS (layout and illustration)
Ink Tank (cover)

A CIP Catalogue record for this book is available from the British Library.

Acknowledgements
This product uses map data licensed from Ordnance Survey © Crown copyright and database rights (2014) Ordnance Survey (100018598). Pages 27, 37, 38, 109, 114 and 115.

The following were adapted from SQA questions with permission, Copyright © Scottish Qualifications Authority: Atmosphere question 1; Hydrosphere questions 1 and 2; Biosphere question 1; Population questions 1 and 2; Urban questions 1 and 2; Development and health questions 1 and 2; Global climate change question 2.

Images
P64 © epa european pressphoto agency b.v. / Alamy; P74 © lbert McCabe / Stringer / Getty Images; P78 Licensed under the Creative Commons Attribution 2.0 Generic license; P108 © UniversalImagesGroup / Contributor / Getty Images.

All other images © Shutterstock.com

Unit 1: Physical Environments

Contents

Unit 2: Human Environments

Unit 3: Global Issues

Atmosphere

In this section

- the global heat budget
- redistribution of energy by atmospheric and oceanic circulation
- cause, characteristics and impact of the Intertropical Convergence Zone (ITCZ)

Take a look at this website for more information:
http://www.georesource.co.uk/atmosphere.html

The Atmosphere is the layer of gases that surround the Earth; consisting mainly of Nitrogen and Oxygen. The other gases, such as Argon and CO_2 are found in much smaller quantities.

The global heat budget

The Earth's surface receives only 56% of the solar energy (or insolation) that reaches the outer atmosphere. To explain this you should use the diagram below.

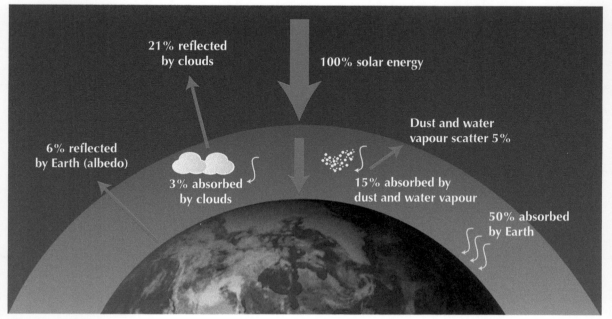

21% reflected by clouds

100% solar energy

Dust and water vapour scatter 5%

6% reflected by Earth (albedo)

3% absorbed by clouds

15% absorbed by dust and water vapour

50% absorbed by Earth

The albedo effect

When explaining why the Earth's surface receives only 56% of the solar energy that reaches the atmosphere, it may be helpful to split your answer into sections.

Clouds

Reflection: 21% of the incoming solar energy is reflected by clouds as they are light in colour. Where there are few clouds there will be less reflection and some clouds also reflect less (e.g. light cirrus clouds – 30%) than others (e.g. heavy cumulonimbus clouds – 90%).

Absorption: only 3% is then absorbed by the clouds, as most of the insolation is reflected.

Dust and gases

Reflection: 5% of the solar insolation is reflected off gas and dust particles.

Absorption: more insolation is absorbed (15%).

This means that only 56% of the initial insolation reaches the Earth's surface.

Earth's surface

Reflection: 6% is reflected due to reflection at the Earth's surface (albedo). Some land surfaces reflect more than others, for example snow reflects 85% and deserts reflect 40%, whereas oceans reflect 10% and forests reflect 15%.

Absorption: the remaining 50% is then absorbed by the Earth.

Global variations in heat energy

Although the Earth, on average, absorbs only 50% of incoming solar energy, there are marked variations in this around the world. The graph below shows that areas within 37 degrees latitude of the Equator receive more solar energy. This is called a positive heat balance. Areas beyond 37 degrees latitude of the Equator absorb less solar energy than they emit energy. This is called negative heat balance.

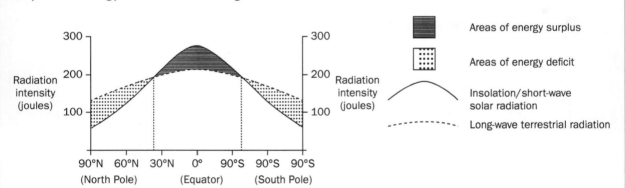

Energy balance and latitude

There are three main reasons to explain why more energy is received at the tropics than the poles:

- Latitude
- Seasons and tilt
- Albedo

TOP TIP

The energy balance graph can appear in a variety of ways (for example vertically). Make sure you can recognise what it shows.

Latitude

The diagram shows that at X (the poles) the sun's rays are much more spread out in comparison to Y (the tropics) where the rays are more concentrated. This means more energy is received at the tropics as there is a smaller surface area.

There is more atmosphere for the rays to travel through at A (the poles) than there is at B (the tropics). This means more insolation is reflected and absorbed before reaching the poles, as it is a larger surface area.

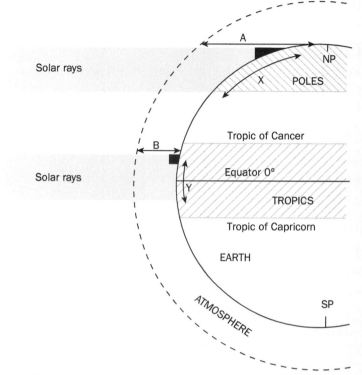

Where the sun's rays reach the Earth

Seasons and tilt

At the tropics, the sun is high in the sky all year round, focusing energy on this area (see Graph A). This means that insolation is high at the tropics all year round and the Equator receives around 12 hours of daylight each day throughout the year. The Tropic of Cancer receives most insolation on June 21st, while the Tropic of Capricorn receives most insolation on December 21st. This is because the Earth tilts, creating seasons.

As the earth is tilted on its axis, the poles receive much less daylight. For example, the North Pole is dark continuously for 6 months and therefore receives no insolation. This can be seen in Graph B.

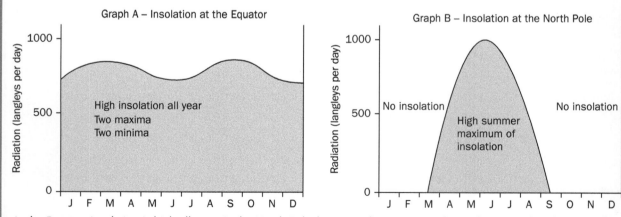

At the Equator, insolation is high all year. At the North Pole, however, there is no insolation for 6 months of the year.

Albedo

In the tropics, more insolation is absorbed because of the increased amount of vegetation, which has a lower albedo. More insolation is reflected at the poles as these have more icy surfaces, which have a higher albedo.

EXAM QUESTION

With the aid of an annotated diagram or diagrams, **explain** why there is a surplus of solar energy in the tropical latitudes and a deficit of solar energy towards the poles.

5 marks

Atmospheric circulation

The air redistributes the energy around the world and this is called atmospheric circulation.

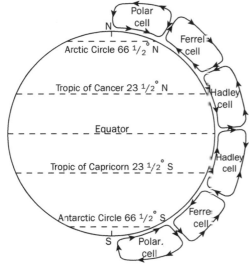

Atmospheric circulation

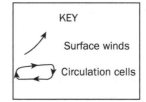

TOP TIP

Students often find this area confusing. Try to learn and understand each cell individually.

KEY	
↗	Surface winds
⬭	Circulation cells

Hadley cell
- On average, the Equator is the hottest area on Earth. Here the air is warm and less dense.
- The warm air rises into the upper atmosphere and spreads out. The rising air forms an area of low pressure called the Equatorial Low.
- As the air spreads out it cools and sinks back to the Earth's surface at 30 degrees north and south of the Equator, forming high pressure called the Sub-Tropical Highs or Horse Highs.
- Some of the air returns to the Equator as the trade winds forming the Hadley cell.

Ferrel cell
- The remaining air blows towards 60 degrees as the mid-latitude westerlies.
- Here the air is heated and rises again, forming another band of low pressure called the Mid-Latitude Low.
- The air spreads again in the upper atmosphere. Some air returns to 30 degrees, completing the Ferrel cell.

Polar cell
- The remaining air moves pole-wards, where it cools and sinks, creating a band of high pressure called the Polar High.
- The air returns back to 60 degrees as the polar easterly winds, completing the Polar cell.

Oceanic circulation

The oceans also redistribute energy around the world. This can be explained by:
- Warm water expands and cold water contracts.
- Warm water moves towards colder areas.
- Cold water is denser than warm water so the cold water sinks away from the poles and spreads towards the Equator.
- The currents are obstructed by continents and can loop, forming gyres.

Case study: Atlantic Ocean

- In the North Atlantic a clockwise loop or gyre is formed when warm water from the Gulf of Mexico (also known as the Gulf Stream) travels northwards.
- The Coriolis effect deflects the currents clockwise in the northern hemisphere and anti-clockwise in the southern hemisphere.
- Prevailing southwesterlies drag the current further north-east. Colder water moves southwards, e.g. the Canaries Current.
- In the South Atlantic, water moves the opposite way than in the North Atlantic. Water moves southwards as the Brazilian Current and is deflected left by the Coriolis force.
- This movement of warm and cold water helps to maintain the energy balance.

TOP TIP

Be aware that there are different case studies you can use and this is just one of them.

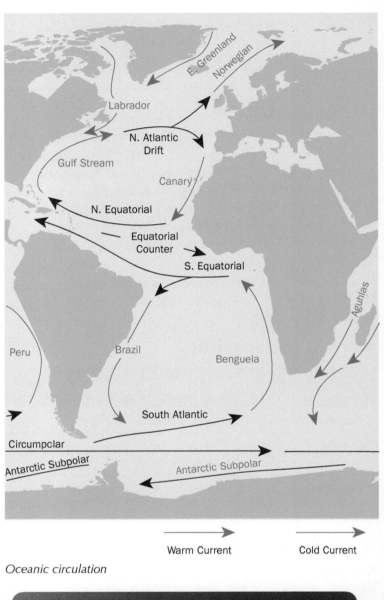

Oceanic circulation

For more on the great ocean conveyor, visit
http://www.bbc.co.uk/programmes/p00gbgmk

Intertropical Convergence Zone (ITCZ)

The Intertropical Convergence Zone (ITCZ) is a band of very low pressure (Equatorial Low). It forms when the southwesterly and northeasterly trade winds meet. The sun is not always overhead at the Equator. At different times of the year the overhead sun moves between the Tropic of Cancer and the Tropic of Capricorn. The ITCZ moves with the overhead sun. In June the ITCZ is over the Tropic of Cancer and in December it is over the Tropic of Capricorn.

TOP TIP

Remember the different characteristics of the air masses. They are easy to remember and can get you quite a few marks!

In West Africa, the ITCZ forms as a result of the Maritime Tropical and the Continental Tropical air masses meeting.

Air mass characteristics

	Maritime Tropical (mT)	**Continental Tropical (cT)**
Name of Wind	South Western Monsoon	Harmattan
Origin	The Atlantic Ocean, in tropical latitudes	The Sahara Desert, in tropical latitudes
Weather	hot/warm, high humidity	hot/very hot, dry, low humidity
Nature	unstable	stable

As a result of the seasonal movement of the ITCZ, rainfall patterns in West Africa vary.

Any country that sits south of the ITCZ will receive the weather brought by the Maritime Tropical air mass, while any country to the north of the ITCZ is affected by weather brought by the Continental Tropical air mass.

When the ITCZ is over the Tropic of Cancer, far more countries are being affected by the Maritime Tropical air mass, and so are experiencing very wet weather. Whereas in December, when the ITCZ is over the Tropic of Capricorn, only coastal areas receive the rainy weather.

When the ITCZ is over the Tropic of Capricorn you will notice in the figure below that it bends round the edges of Western Africa. This is because land heats up much quicker than water and so it follows the land rather than going into the Atlantic Ocean.

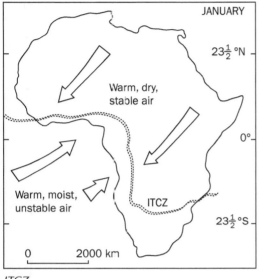 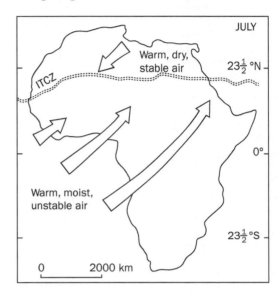

ITCZ

Explaining differences in rainfall in West Africa

Differences in rainfall in West Africa can be attributed to the ITCZ and the movement of the Tropical Maritime and Tropical Continental air masses over the course of the year. Below you will find maps and tables in the style often found in Higher Georgaphy exam papers alongside a question on the ITCZ.

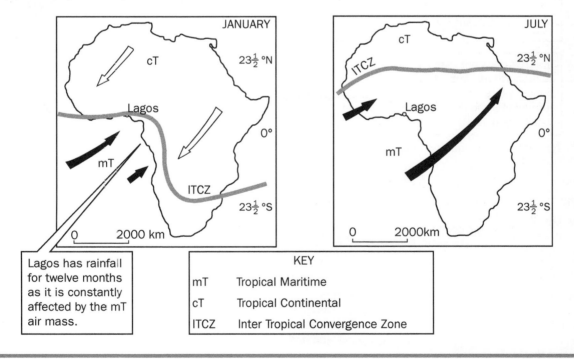

Lagos has rainfall for twelve months as it is constantly affected by the mT air mass.

KEY

mT	Tropical Maritime
cT	Tropical Continental
ITCZ	Inter Tropical Convergence Zone

	J	F	M	A	M	J	J	A	S	O	N	D
Lagos	36	41	132	163	290	452	294	53	154	200	66	28
Jos	3	4	19	98	182	200	302	296	222	46	4	1
Timbuktu	0	0	3	0	3	25	80	82	50	3	0	0

Jos and Timbuktu have distinct dry seasons as they are affected by the cT air mass.

In Lagos, the twin peaks of rainfall in June and October are as a result of the ITCZ migrating north and south with the overhead sun.

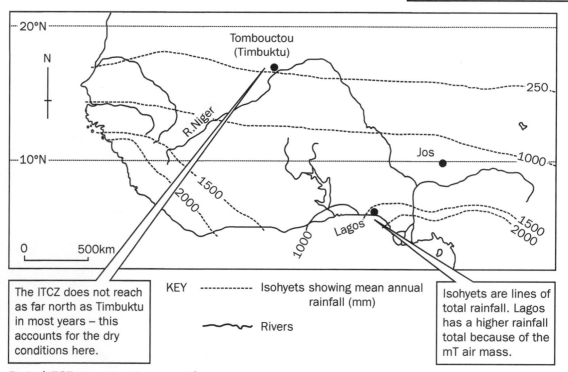

The ITCZ does not reach as far north as Timbuktu in most years – this accounts for the dry conditions here.

KEY

------- Isohyets showing mean annual rainfall (mm)

～～～ Rivers

Isohyets are lines of total rainfall. Lagos has a higher rainfall total because of the mT air mass.

Typical ITCZ exam question materials

TOP TIPS

- The ITCZ does not 'move up and down'. Rather, refer to it as 'migrating north and south'.
- Use all of the diagrams provided as they will often show different things.
- Read the figures from the graphs or tables that are provided. Remember to include these in your answer to fully explain how the rainfall varies.
- Take each place mentioned in turn (there are often three to write about).

GOT IT? ☐ ☐ ☐

Hydrosphere

Hydrosphere

In this section

- hydrological cycle within a drainage basin
- interpretation of hydrographs

Hydrological cycle (or water cycle)

There is a finite amount of water on the planet, this means that no water can be added or lost. However, water does constantly move between the oceans and the atmosphere. This means that the Global Hydrological Cycle is a closed system.

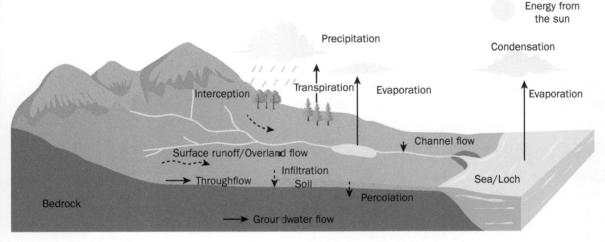

- Evaporation: moisture loss into the atmosphere from water surfaces, soil and vegetation.

- Transpiration: moisture loss through stomata (pores) in plant/tree leaves.

- Interception: raindrops are caught by vegetation before reaching the ground.

- Stemflow: raindrops then either drip off the leaves or flow down tree trunks or stems.

- Throughflow: The movement of water through soil towards the sea or river.

- Infiltration: the passage of water from the ground surface vertically into the soil layer.

- Goundwater: water stored in the pore spaces within a rock.

- Channel flow: the collection of water from rain directly falling in the channel, from surface runoff and from groundwater flow.

The hydrological cycle

The drainage basin

A drainage basin, on the other hand, is an open system, meaning it has inputs and outputs. A drainage basin is an area of land surrounding a river and its tributaries into which all the water drains. It will also include water that is stored in the water table and that flows over the surface as runoff. All rivers have an imaginary line, called a watershed, surrounding the land from which they receive water. When precipitation falls inside the watershed it will find its way into the river. If it falls outside of the watershed it will drain into a different river.

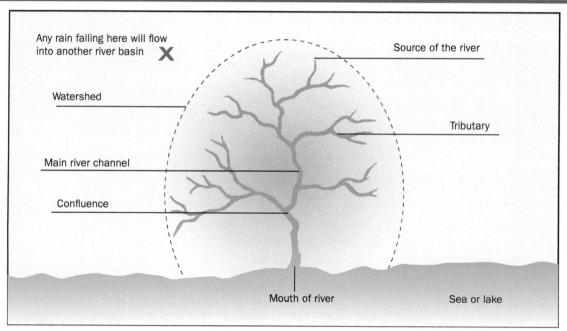

Any rain falling here will flow into another river basin **X**

Source of the river

Watershed

Tributary

Main river channel

Confluence

Mouth of river

Sea or lake

The drainage basin

The drainage basin hydrological cycle is an open system, where water is added and lost and constantly moves around. We say that the drainage basin hydrological cycle has inputs, outputs, stores and transfers.

Inputs	Outputs	Stores	Transfers
Precipitation	Evaporation	Rivers	Overland flow/ Surface runoff
Solar energy	Transpiration	Lakes	Infiltration
	Flowing into sea	Glaciers	Stem flow
		Soil	Through flow
		Groundwater	Percolation
		Vegetation	

Physical factors affecting the hydrological cycle

The journey water takes as it transfers from one part of the hydrological cycle to another will be different in different locations around the world. Some of the physical factors causing these differences are shown in the diagram below:

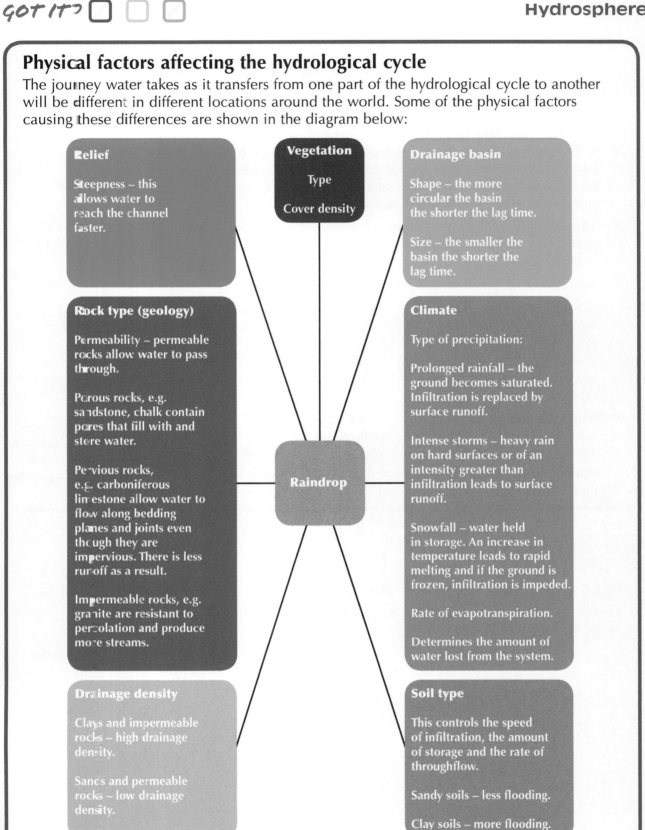

Relief

Steepness – this allows water to reach the channel faster.

Vegetation

Type

Cover density

Drainage basin

Shape – the more circular the basin the shorter the lag time.

Size – the smaller the basin the shorter the lag time.

Rock type (geology)

Permeability – permeable rocks allow water to pass through.

Porous rocks, e.g. sandstone, chalk contain pores that fill with and store water.

Pervious rocks, e.g. carboniferous limestone allow water to flow along bedding planes and joints even though they are impervious. There is less runoff as a result.

Impermeable rocks, e.g. granite are resistant to percolation and produce more streams.

Raindrop

Climate

Type of precipitation:

Prolonged rainfall – the ground becomes saturated. Infiltration is replaced by surface runoff.

Intense storms – heavy rain on hard surfaces or of an intensity greater than infiltration leads to surface runoff.

Snowfall – water held in storage. An increase in temperature leads to rapid melting and if the ground is frozen, infiltration is impeded.

Rate of evapotranspiration.

Determines the amount of water lost from the system.

Drainage density

Clays and impermeable rocks – high drainage density.

Sands and permeable rocks – low drainage density.

Soil type

This controls the speed of infiltration, the amount of storage and the rate of throughflow.

Sandy soils – less flooding.

Clay soils – more flooding.

Factors affecting the passage of a raindrop

Human factors resulting in interference to the hydrological cycle

There are a number of human activities that can interfere with the natural inputs, transfers and storage within a drainage basin:

- **Forestry**: increases interception.
- **Urbanisation**: the removal of natural vegetation to be replaced with impermeable surfaces such as concrete and drains can speed up overland flow and can lead to higher river levels. It also decreases the amount of water returning to groundwater storage, possibly reducing the water table.
- **Mining**: this might lead to a reduction in vegetation cover leading to increased runoff. Lakes, rivers and reservoirs may become silted up, leading to reduced storage capacity in these areas.
- **Deforestation**: the cutting down of trees increases runoff, decreases evapotranspiration and leads to extreme river flows as water is not intercepted and stored by trees.
- **Reservoirs/dam building**: interfering with the natural path of water can change the cycle quite dramatically. Building dams and reservoirs means less water is going underground and therefore stored underground. More surface water means increased evaporation and cloud forming, which may ultimately affect rainfall patterns.
- **Irrigation**: taking water from a river or underground store can reduce the river flow, lower water tables and increase evaporation by placing water in surface stores or by crops removing water from the cycle as they grow.

TOP TIP

Practice drawing the hydrological cycle and become familiar with all the labels and their meanings.

EXAM QUESTION

'A drainage basin is an open system with four elements – inputs, storage, transfers and outputs.'

Explain the movement of water within a drainage basin with reference to the four elements above.

5 marks

Hydrographs

Hydrographs are a visual and graphical means of showing the discharge of a river at a given point over a short period of time.

It is important to understand how a river within a drainage basin will react to a period of rainfall as this can help predict whether a river will cope, or whether it will lead to flooding.

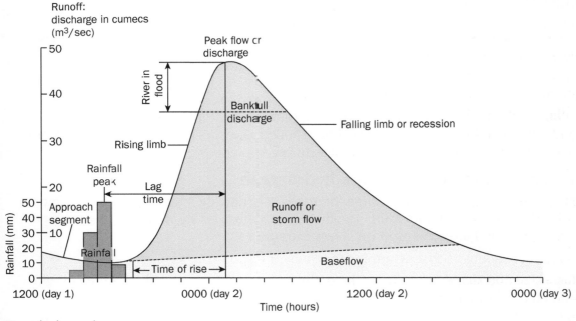

Storm hydrograph

The diagram shows a typical hydrograph. The line graph shows the discharge of a river (volume of water in the channel) and the bar graph shows the rainfall. Along the base of the graph is the time, which may be in hours or days.

When interpreting a hydrograph you must mention some key terminology:

- **Peak flow/discharge:** occurs when the river reaches its highest level (shown by the highest point in the line graph).

- **Peak rainfall:** maximum rainfall (shown by the tallest bar).

Use this link to find out more information on how to interpret hydrographs.
http://www.bbc.co.uk/education/guides/zpqwwmn/revision

- **Lag time**: the time between peak rainfall and peak discharge (it takes time for the rainwater to work its way over and under the ground to the gauging station where the discharge is measured).

- **Rising limb**: the steepness of the line graph indicates the speed at which the rainfall reaches the river. A very steep 'limb' is caused by rapid surface runoff reaching the river all at once.

- **Falling limb**: the line graph as the river returns to normal. River discharge falls more gradually than it rises. Slower throughflow and groundwater flow feed the river more gradually and continuously than surface runoff.

TOP TIP

If you are asked to **describe** a hydrograph you must make sure that you include all of these points:
- What time did is start raining?
- When was peak rainfall? How many millimeters?
- When did it stop raining?
- When did the discharge start to rise?
- What time was peak discharge? How many cumecs?
- What is the lag time?
- When did the discharge return to normal?

Factors affecting the shape of a hydrograph

In some drainage basins river discharge increases very quickly after a storm, which may lead to sudden, devastating flooding. In other drainage basins the impact of a storm is absorbed better and a river's response is less extreme.

There are several factors that determine the level of response:

- **Basin size and shape**: the smaller the drainage basin the more likely the rainfall will reach the river more quickly.

- **Relief and slope**: in steep-sided upland valleys water is more likely to reach the river quickly than in gently sloping areas.

- **Types of precipitation**: prolonged rainfall will cause saturated ground, so rainwater will run over the surface and into the channel quickly, leading to a shorter lag time and higher peak discharge.

- **Rock type**: if the water falls onto an impermeable surface, the water will run over the land as surface runoff and will reach the river faster. Alternatively, if the rain falls onto a permeable surface it will be infiltrated into the ground, which is a much slower process.

- **Land use:** dense vegetation cover will help by intercepting rainfall and this will lengthen lag times. Tropical rainforests intercept 80% of rainfall, arable land only 10%. Short lag times and high peak discharge are most likely to occur on bare ground surface such as deforested areas.

- **Temperature:** extremes of temperature can restrict infiltration, e.g. permafrost or baked desert soils.

- **Soil type**: clay soils will act as an impermeable barrier and rain will run off, whereas with sandy soils infiltration will be greater so lag times will be longer.

- **Urbanisation:** these areas tend to be covered in impermeable rock such as tarmac and concrete, therefore the water will run over the land and reach the river quickly.

TOP TIP

If you are asked to **explain** a hydrograph you must make sure you mention the factors above.

Basin lag time

The basin lag time (the time it takes for the rainfall to reach the river) depends on how fast or slow the processes are.

Fast processes	Slow processes
Overland flow	Infiltration
Surface runoff	Percolation
	Throughflow

The difference between describing and explaining a hydrograph

We can describe and explain this hydrograph as follows:

Description

- What time did it start raining?
  02.00 on 29th April.
- When was peak rainfall? How many millimetres?
  06.00 on 29th April, when 3.75mm of rain fell.
- When did it stop raining?
  17.00 on 29th April.
- When did the discharge start to rise?
  03.00 on 29th April.
- What time was peak discharge? How many cumecs?
  09.00 when the river levels reached 73cms.
- What is the lag time?
  3 hours.
- When did the discharge return to normal?
  River levels fall to 42cm on 30th April.

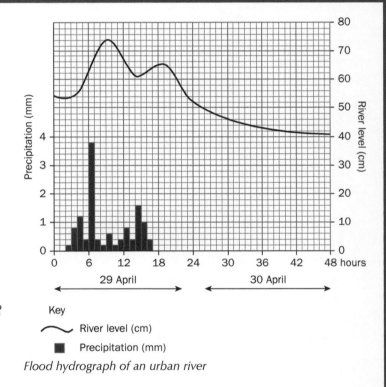

Key
~ River level (cm)
■ Precipitation (mm)

Flood hydrograph of an urban river

Explanation

- The rising limb is quite steep and the lag time is short at only 3 hours, which shows that the rainfall reached the river very quickly. This could be due to it being an urbanized area; therefore the rainfall will run over the land as surface runoff and into the river.
- As this is a town, there is likely to be little vegetation to intercept the rainfall.
- There will be little soil cover, therefore rainfall will not be infiltrated.
- Plenty of impermeable surfaces such as concrete will increase runoff.
- The river basin may be small, allowing the rainfall to reach the river quickly.

EXAM QUESTION

Explain the changing river levels on the River Thaw at Cowbridge on 26th July 2007.

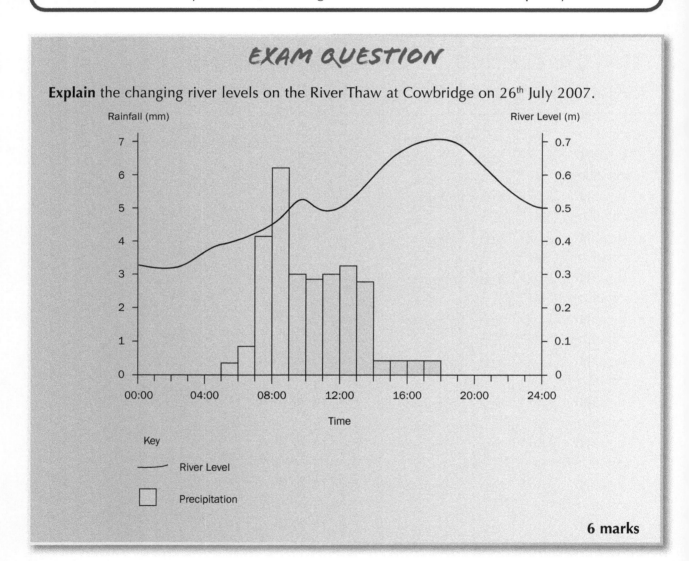

Key

—— River Level

☐ Precipitation

6 marks

Lithosphere

In this section

- **the formation of erosion and depositional features in glaciated and coastal landscapes**
- **rural land use conflicts and their management in a glaciated and coastal area**

Visit **http://www.georesource.co.uk/glaciation1.html** for more photos and information on the glaciation topic.

Glaciation

The average temperature of the Earth has varied in cycles. These are known as 'ice ages' and 'inter-glacial' periods. During the last Ice Age, much of the landscape of the United Kingdom was shaped and these features still exist today. There are many areas of the world that are still subject to glacial erosion and deposition, including the Alps, the Himalayas and the Andes.

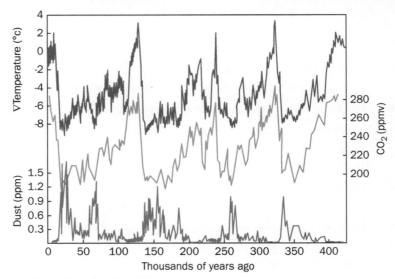

Readings from the Vostok ice core

For more on this, take a look at this video on Ice Age Cycles: **http://www.bbc.co.uk/science/earth/water_and_ice/ice_age#p00gtnlg**

Erosional features

For the exam you must be able to draw, annotate and provide a paragraph or so to explain the formation of various features of glacial erosion and deposition.

Erosional features are those that have been carved out by the ice.

TOP TIP

Providing named examples can allow you to gain extra marks.

Corrie, e.g. north-eastern side of Helvellyn

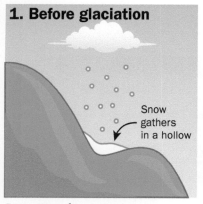
1. Before glaciation
Snow gathers in a hollow

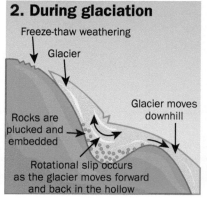
2. During glaciation
Freeze-thaw weathering
Glacier
Rocks are plucked and embedded
Glacier moves downhill
Rotational slip occurs as the glacier moves forward and back in the hollow

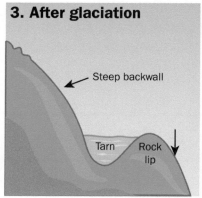
3. After glaciation
Steep backwall
Tarn
Rock lip

Formation of a corrie

- Snow collects in a hollow, which is often at a high altitude and north-facing as these areas are colder. The snow then **compresses, turning to firn/neve, then ice.**
- Due to gravity, this ice then moves downhill as a glacier.
- **Freeze-thaw** weathering **erodes** the back of the hollow. This is when meltwater enters cracks in the rock, freezes and expands by 9%. This forces the crack wider and when this has happened many times over the rock will break apart.
- **Plucking** (when the glacier freezes onto the rock and plucks away the loose rock) occurs as it moves down the mountainside. This makes the backwall much steeper.
- The base of the hollow becomes deeper through **abrasion** (where pieces of rock, embedded in the bottom of the glacier, scrape and wear down the rock underneath as the glacier moves).
- After the ice melts an armchair shaped hollow is left in the mountainside; this is a **corrie**. A **lip** is found where less pressure is exerted by the glacier, or there has been a temporary loss of energy and the glacier has had to deposit. Water can sometimes gather in the hollow and this is known as a **corrie lochan or tarn.**

GOT IT? ☐ ☐ ☐

Arête, e.g. Striding Edge

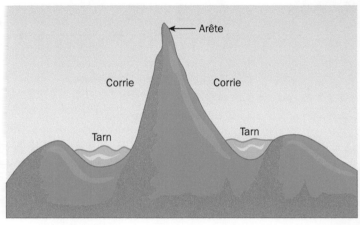

Striding Edge in the Lake District

Formation of an arête

To explain the formation of an arête you should write out the formation of a corrie first. At the end you should include: after the ice melts, two armchair shaped hollows, or corries, are left in the mountainside; the knife-edged ridge in between these is an arête.

Pyramidal peak

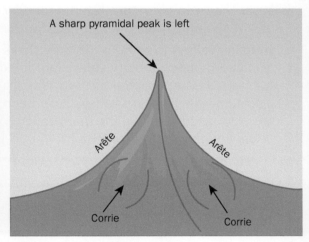

The Matterhorn

Formation of a pyramidal peak

To explain the formation of a pyramidal peak you should write out the formation of a corrie first. At the end you should include: after the ice melts three or more armchair shaped hollows, or corries, are left in the mountainside; the highest point in the centre is called a pyramidal peak.

U-shaped valley (e.g. Great Langdale) and hanging valley (e.g. Little Langdale)

1. Before glaciation

Tributary

Main river

2. During glaciation
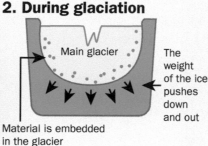

Main glacier

Material is embedded in the glacier

The weight of the ice pushes down and out

3. After glaciation
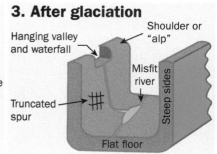

Hanging valley and waterfall

Shoulder or "alp"

Misfit river

Truncated spur

Steep sides

Flat floor

Formation of a U-shaped valley and a hanging valley

- Before glaciation a river runs through a **V-shaped river valley**. **Freeze-thaw** weathering weakens the rocks at the sides and base of the valley. This is when water enters the cracks in the rock. At night, when temperatures drop below zero degrees, the water freezes and expands (by as much as 9%). During the day when temperatures rise, the ice melts and releases the pressure. This is a continuous process that causes the rock to become very weak and break off.

- During glaciation, a glacier moves through the V-shaped valley. As it does so it pulls huge amounts of rocks away from the sides and base of the valley (known as **plucking**). **Abrasion** occurs when small rocks that are embedded inside the glacier scrape against the rocks, smoothing them like sandpaper. This deepens the base.

- After glaciation a huge valley is left with very steep sidewalls and a very wide, flat base. The river will return but it no longer 'fits' the wide valley and so is known as a **'misfit stream'**. **Scree** often collects at the base of the valley sides due to weathering.

- **Hanging valleys** form from tributary rivers that flow into the main river below. During glaciation, these tributary valleys are filled with small glaciers. These glaciers do not have the same power as the valley glacier and so do less vertical erosion. After glaciation, the tributary valleys have been cut off by the main valley glacier and so are left 'hanging' above the main valley. When the rivers return, the hanging valley is usually marked with a waterfall.

Depositional features

Depositional features are formed by the ice 'dumping' material.

Terminal moraine
- Moraine is the material that is carried by the glacier.
- Terminal moraines form when the ice loses energy and deposits all the moraine it was carrying.
- This might be when the glacier reaches flat land or when it begins to melt.
- The moraine is deposited at the front (snout) of the glacier.
- The longer that the ice continues to melt, the higher the terminal moraine.

- Terminal moraines are completely unsorted; they are made up of all the material that the glacier carries and soil and rock that it 'bulldozed' in front of it.
- Terminal moraines can extend for many kilometres.
- They mark the furthest point reached by the glacier.

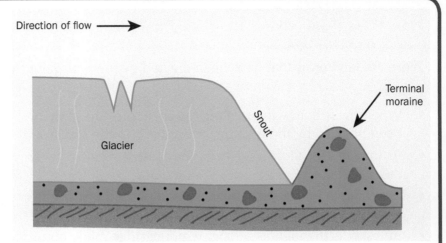

Formation of a terminal moraine

Drumlin, Glasgow has been built on a number of drumlins

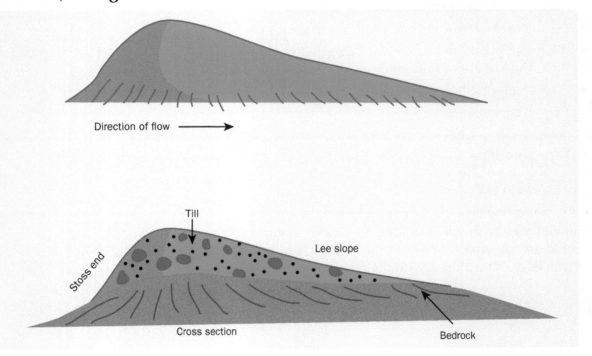

Formation of a drumlin

- This is a feature of deposition made up of unsorted boulder clay/till (deposits from the ice sheet).
- The drumlin would have been deposited when the glacier became overloaded with sediment.
- The stoss end is steeper and refers to the side facing uphill.
- The lee slope is gently sloping and faces down the valley. This is because the glacier moves over an outcrop of bedrock and dumps material, before smoothing over the top.
- These are normally found in groups, known as swarms.
- They can be 1 km long and 500 metres wide.
- Glaciologists still disagree as to exactly how they were formed.

Fluvio-glacial features

These are landforms that have been created by the meltwater from ice sheets and glaciers.

Eskers

- When rivers below the melting ice sheet pick up some of the loose material that has been plucked by the ice, they transport it to the snout of the glacier.
- As they move out the ice sheet, they lose power and energy and, as a result, deposit the material.
- Larger particles are heavier and are deposited first. Therefore the deposits that make up an esker are sorted.
- An esker is then left as a long, winding ridge made up of moraine.

Outwash plain

- Terminal moraine marks the furthest point of the glacial advance. Meltwater from the glacier picks up pieces of rock.
- As the meltwater loses energy, it has to deposit.
- Outwash plains are sorted, the larger materials are heavier and therefore are dumped first. These materials are often quite rounded by the process of attrition.
- The smaller particles are dumped last and therefore will be more rounded.

Glaciated uplands on an Ordnance Survey (OS) map

You will also be required to identify various features of glacial erosion on a map. You should be able to identify lots of different features. The figures that follow show some examples of 3D features, with their associated contour pattern.

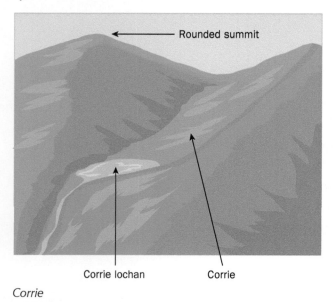
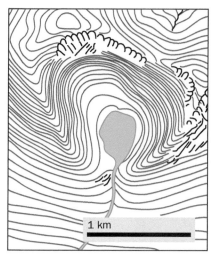

Corrie

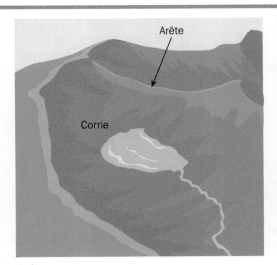

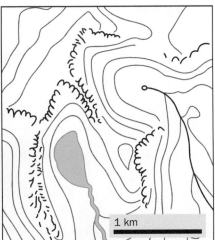

Arête

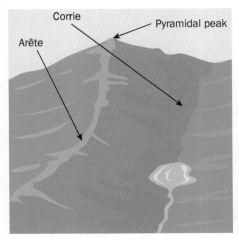

Pyramidal peak

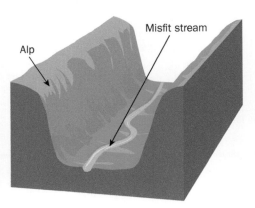

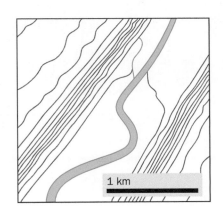

U-shaped valley

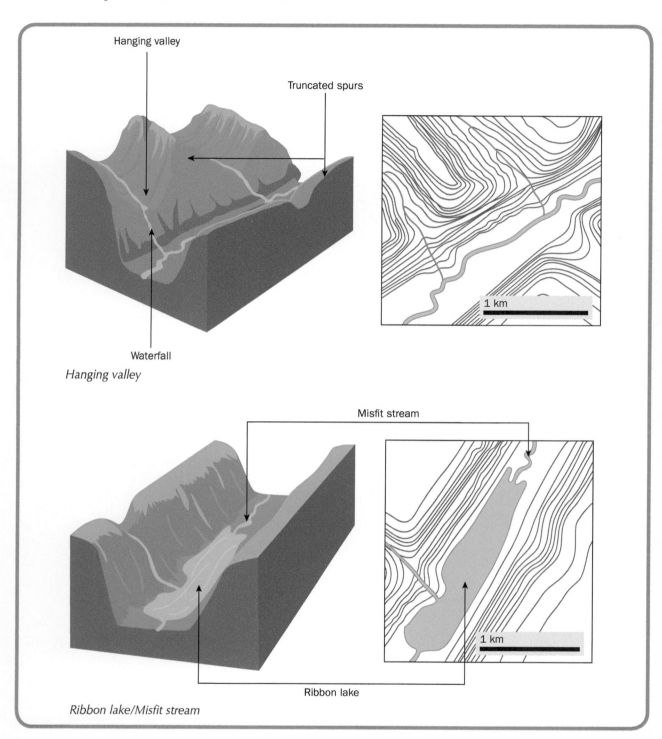

Hanging valley

Truncated spurs

Waterfall

1 km

Hanging valley

Misfit stream

Ribbon lake

1 km

Ribbon lake/Misfit stream

The map below shows an area of the Cairngorms. There are some hints below to help you identify features.

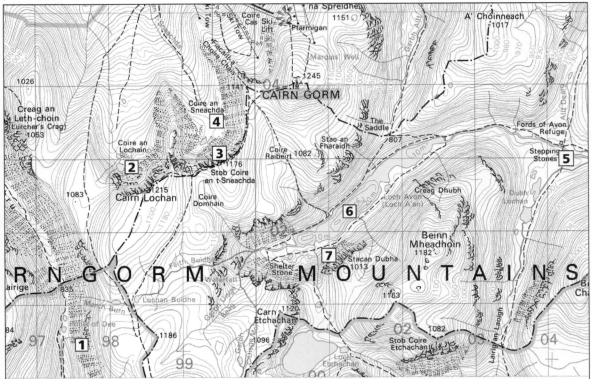

Features identified on an OS map

1. Scree: Look out for the small dots on the map. It is found at the bottom of steep slopes.

2. Corrie Lochan: Coloured blue and found in a corrie – they are often named.

3. Arête: Look for a knife-edged ridge between two corries. Often surrounded by scree.

4. Corrie: These are often named so look out for the words Coire and Cwm. The contour lines are also horse-shoe shaped.

5. U-shaped Valley: Look for white space surrounded by contour lines which are very close together.

6. Ribbon Lake: Look for large bodies of water at the bottom of the valley.

7. Truncated Spur: This is where an interlocking spur is cut off. Look for exposed rock and scree at the side of the valley.

Other hints

U-shaped valleys often contain a misfit stream surrounded by flat (white on the map) land. Look out for roads as these are often built on the valley floor.

Pyramidal peaks are surrounded by three or more corries. Look out for a height at the top that signifies a peak, although not always a pyramidal one.

Truncated spurs can be difficult to spot. Look out for rock outcrops at the side of U-shaped valleys.

Hanging valleys are perpendicular to the main valley. Keep an eye out for waterfalls.

EXAM QUESTION

Explain, with the aid of an annotated diagram or diagrams, how an arête is formed.

5 marks

Rural land use conflicts: The Lake District

The Lake District is England's largest national park and is home to Scafell Pike, Wastwater and thriving communities like Keswick and Bowness-on-Windermere. The area is enjoyed by over 15 million visitors every year due to its accessible location and beautiful scenery.

TOP TIP

Remember to stick with one case study. The exam will always allow you to refer to 'an area you have studied'.

An aerial photograph of the Lake District

There are several conflicts that occur as a result of the large volume of tourists visiting the region. The following tables illustrate these conflicts.

Traffic congestion

Conflicts	Solutions	Effectiveness
The many visitors arriving at the Lake District often travel by car. There are bottlenecks in Bowness and Ambleside that often cause **traffic congestion**.	**Boat shuttles**, e.g. Bowness to Hawkeshead on Windermere have been introduced to reduce congestion on the roads.	This has been a success as the **Cross Lakes Shuttle service** is growing in popularity and has been extended to other lakes in an effort to reduce traffic.
Congestion on the narrow, winding roads causes **access problems** for locals and the emergency services.	Proposals have been forwarded to reopen the Keswick to Penrith **railway** and to increase services on the Windermere branch line.	However, it would be **impractical financially** and also extremely difficult to extend the railway in the Lakes given the **relief of the land**.

Conflicts	Solutions	Effectiveness
A **lack of parking facilities** means that cars often park on the roadside and use 'unofficial car parks'. This creates further congestion as traffic cannot freely move through the roads. Grass verges have also become badly eroded as cars are left at the roadside.	**Grasmere now offers no on-street parking** to reduce congestion, and Keswick Main Street has been **pedestrianised** with car parks found on the edge. Some villages have set up **restricted parking zones**, for example in Elterwater. The car park on the edge of the village has been expanded and parking on grass verges and near houses has been restricted.	**Traffic continues to be a problem**, especially in areas such as Grasmere, which has one of the highest levels of parking fines issued in the UK. This is due to the increasing number of visitors to the area but also the ever-increasing car ownership figures. This is an extremely difficult problem to overcome as there is only one train station in the area, which is far from the main village.
Locals conducting their everyday business often experience **problems such as getting from place to place** and crossing the road. Pollution has reached dangerous levels in certain areas.	**Public transport** has been **improved and subsidised**, for example the 'Langdale Rambler' bus service. Visitors are encouraged to use the buses instead of bringing their cars into the national park.	

Footpath erosion

Conflicts	Solutions	Effectiveness
Many visitors use the footpaths in the area. They sometimes stray from the paths or walk on the edge, which leads to **footpath erosion**. In turn, this **scars** the landscape, e.g. Brown Tongue to Scaffel. There are currently around **200 paths in need of repair** and this is an **expensive and time-consuming** job.	**Tourist guides have been produced that do not include various areas** in order to reduce pressure on them, e.g. Brown Tongue to Scafell and Tarn Hoes. **Physical barriers** such as **fencing** and **vegetation** are used in some areas to stop footpath erosion. Also, the Lake District National Park is working with landowners such as the National Trust to **provide pitched surfaces**, reseeding and construction of drainage channels.	Due to the vast number of visitors, footpath erosion is an **ongoing problem** with approximately 200 paths in the Lake District in need of repair.  *Example of footpath erosion*

Holiday homes and second homes

Conflicts	Solutions	Effectiveness
Many houses and other types of accommodation have become **second homes** (around 20% in the Lake District), bought by wealthy people from the cities, and these can lie empty for a large part of the season. This causes **house prices to inflate** and locals are then forced out as they cannot afford the costs. **Various local services such as primary schools** (Ulpha Primary) then **close** as those who own the second homes do not need to use the services.	The **'Rothswaite Scheme'** (Borrowdale) attempted to ensure some properties were **available for locals** and not lost to second home owners. To qualify you had to have lived or worked in the area for at least three years.	While the scheme was successful, it was **on too small a scale**.  *A holiday home in the Lake District*

Farmers

Conflicts	Solutions
Many **walkers do not follow the country code**, which upsets farmers.	Conflicts between tourists and farmers have been addressed by tourist information centres, which offer free **guided walks, talks, newsletters** and an **updated website** to **raise awareness of the country code**.
Walkers can unintentionally leave gates open and farm animals can escape.	
People throw **their litter**, making the area look less appealing. **Animals** may also **ingest the rubbish**, which can cause them to choke.	
Walkers can unintentionally **damage stonewalls** by carelessly climbing over them. This all contributes to the farmer losing money.	

Use of the lakes

Conflicts	Solutions	Effectiveness
Watersports create waves, which in turn cause **erosion** of the shoreline.	A **speed limit** was introduced on Lake Windermere.  *The lakes are used for many different water sports*	Conservationists welcomed the new speed limit, but speedboat owners, water skiers, and boat companies around the lake objected to the change. **Businesses have been affected** and boat users have had to find alternative lakes.
Loud noises from the watersports can also **scare fish**, which means fishermen are often in conflict with those who participate in noisy water sports.		
Some boats can cause **water pollution** and this affects those wanting to swim in the area.		

Coasts

Coastlines are constantly changing. There are three key coastal processes:

- **Erosion:** as the waves move, they wear away the coastline. They do this by using a combination of processes (these are explained in the next section).
- **Transportation:** the movement of material by the waves.
- **Deposition:** when the waves run out of energy, material is dumped.

Coastal erosion

There are many factors that determine the shape of a coastline including: climate, rock type, tides, volcanic activity and wave frequency. Waves are the most effective agent of erosion along the coastline. They are created by wind blowing over the surface of the sea. Their size is determined by the fetch (the distance over which the wave has travelled), the wind speed and the depth of the water.

Constructive waves	Destructive waves
Strong swash pushes material up the beach Weak backwash Rebuilds beaches Smaller in height Gentle beach slope	Weak swash little beach building Strong backwash Sharper beach slope Waves scour the beach pulling sand and shingle down the beach

Constructive and destructive waves

The sea erodes in four ways and produces various features of erosion. The four main processes of coastal erosion are:

- **Hydraulic action:** waves crash against a cliff and drive water under great pressure into cracks in the rock. This pressure squeezes the air, and as the wave falls back the air expands explosively, loosening pieces of rock.
- **Corrasion:** corrasion (or abrasion) occurs when stones and pebbles are picked up by waves and thrown against the cliff, causing erosion.
- **Attrition:** rock fragments (stones and pebbles) hit against each other and so are reduced in size.
- **Solution:** salty sea water chemically dissolves rocks. This is most noticeable on chalk and limestone cliffs.

There are various features that have been formed through coastal erosion. You must be able to explain how those listed on the following pages are formed.

Cliffs and wave-cut platforms, e.g. Durlston Cliffs and Kimmeridge Bay

Photograph of wave-cut platform

- At high tide and during storms, waves erode cliffs at their base using hydraulic action, corrosion and solution. This forms a wave cut notch that eventually turns into a cave.
- The rock becomes unstable and cracks begin to appear. Vertical cracks may eventually reach the top of the cliff, creating a blowhole.
- The cliff is then unstable and collapses due to gravity.
- As the cliff retreats, a wave-cut

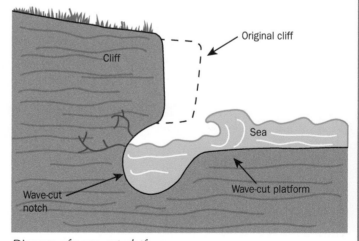

Diagram of wave-cut platform

platform is left. This is an area of flat land that juts out into the sea. The whole process repeats and the cliff retreats further.

Headlands and bays, e.g. Swanage Bay

- Where there are different bands of rock, the coast is liable to differential erosion.

- Softer, less resistant rock is eroded more quickly through the processes of hydraulic action (the force of the waves against the rock), corrosion (when stones and pebbles are picked up by waves and thrown against the cliff, causing erosion) and solution (when the salty sea water chemically dissolves the rock)

- The harder, more resistant rock is not eroded as quickly and 'sticks out' as a headland.

- Because the headland sticks out, it is subject to the highest energy waves. The bays though are sheltered and receive low energy waves that deposit rather than erode.

- This then means that the coastline becomes straight again.

1.

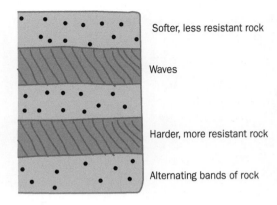

Softer, less resistant rock

Waves

Harder, more resistant rock

Alternating bands of rock

2.

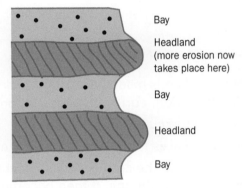

Bay

Headland (more erosion now takes place here)

Bay

Headland

Bay

Formation of headlands and bays

Caves (e.g. Tilly Whim Caves), arches (e.g. Durdle Door), stacks (e.g. Old Harry Rocks) and stumps

The Old Harry Rocks, in Dorset

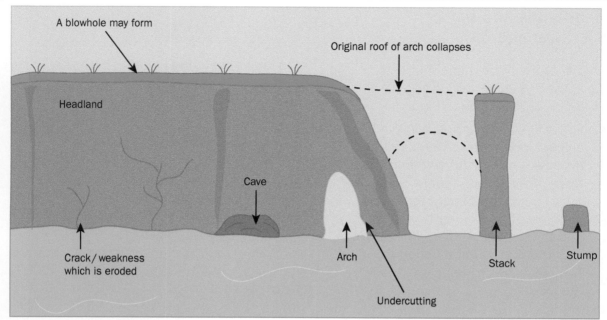

Formation of caves, arches and stacks

- When headlands made of resistant rock are attacked by waves, the processes of hydraulic action, corrosion and solution occur.
- A cliff is undercut, forming a cave.
- When two caves form back-to-back, they meet to form an arch.
- The rock above the arch is now subject to hydraulic action by storm waves and to freeze-thaw weathering. It then becomes unstable and collapses due to gravity.
- This leaves a rock that is separated from the headland, called a stack.
- A stack will continue to be attacked by wave action and by physical and chemical weathering and is eventually worn down to sea level, leaving a stump.

Coastal transportation: longshore drift

When waves approach the coast, they do so at an angle because of the direction of the prevailing wind. Swash carries the material onto the beach, while backwash allows material to flow back to the sea at 90 degrees. As this process of transportation repeatedly occurs, material moves in a zigzag fashion along the coast. This movement of material is called longshore drift.

Longshore drift is explained in bite-sized form here: **http://www.bbc.co.uk/learningzone/clips/coastlines-longshore-drift/8440.html**

Coastal deposition

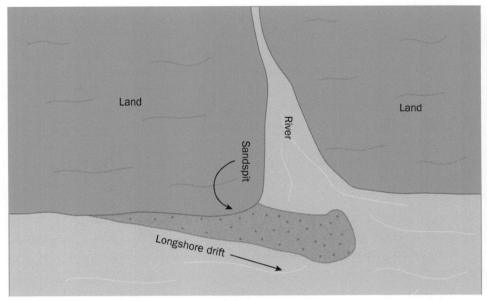

This diagram shows the formation of sandspits

Sandspits/tombolos/bars

- Material is transported via the process of longshore drift along the coastline (where swash and backwash transport and deposit material).
- Where the coastline changes direction, the material will be deposited in open water.
- This material eventually builds up to above sea level and forms a sandspit (which is an extension to the beach).
- As the sandspit becomes longer, its rate of growth decreases because the water either becomes deeper, or the width of the channel is decreased and so the current becomes faster.
- If the sandspit connects with an island it becomes a tombolo.
- If the sandspit connects with another piece of land across an inlet, it becomes a bar. A lagoon is often found behind a bar that will eventually fill with sediment and dry up.

A tombolo

Beach

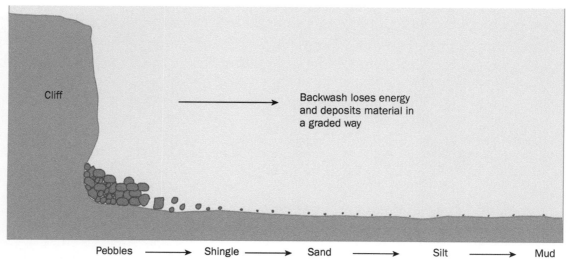

Cliff

Backwash loses energy and deposits material in a graded way

Pebbles ──→ Shingle ──→ Sand ──→ Silt ──→ Mud

How a beach is formed

- Beaches are found in areas where the deposition of sand and shingle is greater than its removal by wave action.
- They are often found in sheltered areas, such as bays, with low energy waves.
- Beach material is deposited by the swash as the waves lose energy.
- The backwash then returns the water to the sea, picking up some beach material.
- As the waves deposit material, the larger particles are dropped first.
- The beach therefore becomes graded, with the sand and silt often carried back into the sea.

Coasts on OS maps

TOP TIP

When sand spits appear on an OS map the direction of the longshore drift can be determined as it will be moving towards where the end of the spit is being formed.

Just like in the Glaciation topic earlier in this chapter, you should be able to identify various coastal features on an OS Map. Here are some of the things you should be looking out for:

- Cliffs
- Wave-cut platforms
- Headlands
- Bays
- Caves
- Arches
- Stacks
- Sand spits
- Lagoons

Small Bay: 'Cove'

Wave cut platform: Look for the rugged edge along the coastline

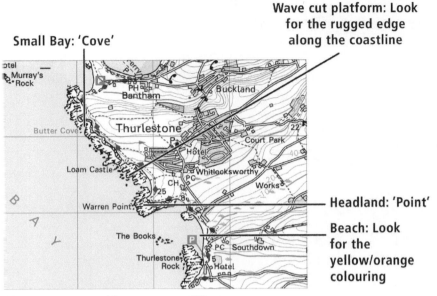

Headland: 'Point'

Beach: Look for the yellow/orange colouring

How to spot coastal features on an OS map

For more on identifying these features, see **http://www.bbc.co.uk/bitesize/higher/geography/physical/lithosphere/revision/3/**

You can see more examples of this here: **http://www.bbc.co.uk/education/guides/zgnhhyc/revision/5**

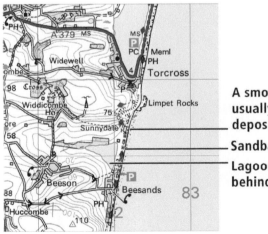

A smooth coastline usually means it is a depositional coastline

Sandbar

Lagoon trapped behind sandbar

More coastal features as they are shown on an OS map

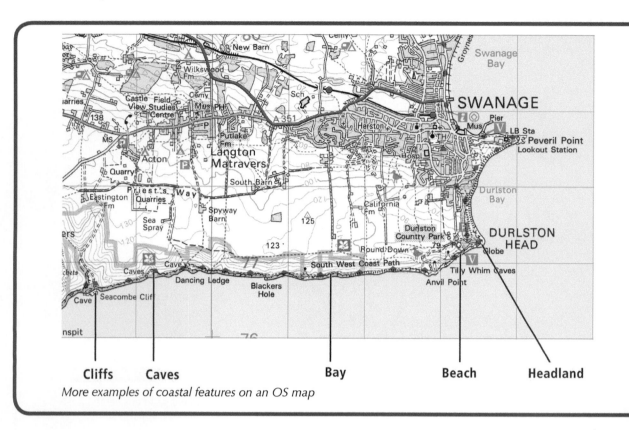

Cliffs Caves Bay Beach Headland

More examples of coastal features on an OS map

Rural land use conflicts: Dorset coast

The Jurassic Coast is England's first natural World Heritage Site. It stretches over 95 miles of coastline from East Devon to Dorset. With millions of visitors every year, many conflicts occur, and these are illustrated in the following tables.

Location of Dorset

Traffic at the outskirts of Bournemouth

Traffic congestion

Conflicts	Solutions	Effectiveness
90% of people visiting the Dorset Coast arrive via **car or coach.**	The **size** of the car park at Lulworth Cove was **increased** and profits from the car park were used to **subsidise a bus service from the local railway station** to encourage people to leave their cars behind. A **park and ride scheme** has been introduced to allow visitors to travel via ferry to Studland Heath from nearby towns to reduce traffic congestion.	Solutions to traffic congestion are **costly**, e.g. bigger or new car parks. Also, conservationists deemed the car park at Lulworth Cove a **'scar on the landscape'**. It has been decided that no more overspill car parks will be built as they are destroying the heath land they are trying to protect. However, with **increasing car ownership** this will **continue to be an area of concern.**
Roughly 500,000 people visit Lulworth Cove in one year.		
Roads are quite often **narrow** and therefore cannot deal with the large volume of traffic.		
Due to the **lack of appropriate parking**, many cars park illegally on the heath land and roadsides.		
This slows the traffic down as they try to pass parked cars on single lane roads.		
Traffic causes both **noise** and **air pollution**.		

The Ministry of Defence

Conflicts	Solution
Some areas of the Dorset Coast are used for **live firing**, which creates **noise**. There are sometimes **restrictions on the movement of visitors**, i.e. when roads or the South West Coastal Path are closed.	A **'no firing' policy** has been implemented on the Lulworth range at **weekends** and **during busy holiday periods**. Roads are also kept open during these times.

Footpath and sand dune erosion

Conflicts	Solutions	Effectiveness
The **South West Coastal Path,** between Lulworth Cove and Durdle Door, is **used by 200,000 people each year.** Many people wander off the footpaths and **destroy the heath land,** while others walk at the edges and widen the path.	**Sections of the path have been moved inland** to ease pressure on the crumbling cliff chalks. **Fences** have been constructed beside some paths so that people do not stray away from them. **Footpaths** are also **designated to follow 'desire lines'.** More **traditional methods of paving,** such as **using local chalk,** have been used so that the paths are more in-keeping with the area.	Footpath erosion **continues to be a problem with the high visitor numbers.** It was particularly unpopular when some paths were moved further inland, away from the sea view that visitors had come to enjoy.
Heavy jeeps are sometimes used for recreational driving on the sand dunes. This **destroys the fragile grasses,** which can then cause dunes to be destabalised.	Various **ditches** have been dug to **prevent jeeps from off-roading** on the heathland. **Fines** have been introduced to motorcyclists found off-roading on the heathland.	

Yachts at the Dorset coast

Conflicting activities

Conflicts	Solutions	Effectiveness
The **loud noises** created by various activities such as jet skiing can disturb and **scare off birds**, and many bird watchers visit the area.	An **'Aquatic Management Plan'** has been introduced to encourage wind surfers to go **further out to sea**.	In Poole Harbour, the **Local Authority is unwilling to ban** speed boats and block access to particular areas as the visitors **bring in money** to the local economy.
Loud noises can also **scare fish** which means fishermen are often in conflict with those who participate in noisy water sports.	**Zoning** has also been introduced to encourage quiet areas, for example for bird watching and fishing.	
Yachts in the bay can cause **water pollution** and this affects those wanting to swim in the area.	There has been an **increase** in the number of **marinas** that have been built to reduce the number of boats moored in the harbour.	

Litter

Conflicts	Solutions	Effectiveness
Like many other busy areas, **litter** remains a problem as tourists do not always bin their rubbish.	Litter has been tackled by **placing more bins** in the area. There have been many **community initiatives to raise awareness** of litter problems. See Dorset's recent education website here: https://www.dorsetforyou.com/litter-free-coast	**Litter remains a problem** at the Dorset Coast, just like other popular areas in Britain.
Dog fouling is a problem on beaches, e.g. Studland Heath.	Dog fouling has been reduced by **banning dogs** on the heathland during the summer months.	

Rural depopulation

Conflicts	Solutions	Effectiveness
Many of the **jobs are seasonal** (mainly only for the summer months) which means that there can be high **unemployment** during winter months. Only 10% of the total number of visitors come to the Dorset Coast from November to February.	**Bournemouth has promoted itself as a business and conference centre** (and is often used for political conferences) to offer all year round employment.	These schemes have proven **popular**, though **house price rises remain to be a problem** in Dorset, as well as many areas in the South of England.
Many houses and other types of accommodation have become **second homes**, bought by wealthy people from the cities, and these can lie empty for a large part of the season. This causes **house prices to inflate** and **locals** are then forced out as they **cannot afford the costs**. House prices in Dorset have risen 97% from 1999–2005. **Various local services** such as primary schools then **close** as those who own the second homes do not need to use these services.	**Graduate recruitment schemes** have been introduced to match graduates with prospective employers and encourage young people to stay in the area. East Dorset District Council are trying to **reduce or end 50% discount on council tax for second home owners.** The **Rural Housing Enablers Scheme** is trying to identify opportunities for development of rural housing and promote affordable housing for local residents; they do this by offering **grants to build low cost housing for residents** and by **identifying new areas to develop**.	

EXAM QUESTION

Explain the conflicts that arise as a result of tourists in a coastal area you have studied.

6 marks

Biosphere

In this section

• properties and formation processes of podzol, brown earth and gley soils

Soils

All forms of life on land depend one way or another on soil. Soil is the thin layer that has formed as a result of all the physical, chemical and biological weathering of the underlying rock (often called parent material) of the Earth's surface. It can vary in depth from a few centimetres to many metres. Yet its formation is slow; typically 1 cm of soil can take between 100–1000 years to form depending on the inputs and outputs.

For Higher you need to be able to describe the characteristics and explain the formation of three zonal soils (brown earths, podzols and gleys) all found in the UK, but also found in similar climates around the world.

You will need to know what the soil profile looks like for each of the soils. A soil profile is a vertical section through a soil (as if you had sliced a spade through the soil until you hit solid rock). Soil profiles are made up of soil horizons – these are distinctive horizontal layers in a soil profile.

Soil formation

The 'ingredients' of soil were identified by the American soil scientist H. Jenny in the following equation:

S= f(CORP)t

Soil is a function of **C** climate, **O** organisms and vegetation, **R** relief, **P** parent material and **t** time.

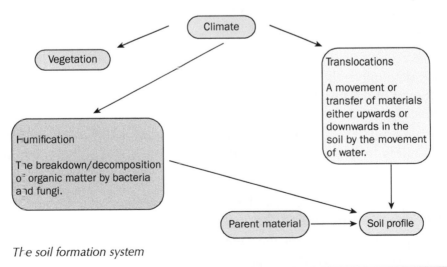

The soil formation system

Soils are made up as follows:

- **45% mineral matter**: this comes from the weathering or breakdown of the underlying parent material. It consists of a range of particle sizes from small clay particles (<0.002mm diameter) to coarse sand (>2mm diameter). The texture of the soil is determined by the particle mix.
- **5% organic matter**: this comes from decaying vegetable matter that is broken down by decomposers, e.g. fungi, earthworms.
- **25% air**
- **25% water**

Definitions of soil processes

Process	Definition
Acidity	A measure of the hydrogen ion concentration in the soil. Values greater than 7.0 are alkaline and values less than 7.0 are acid.
Capillary action	Transfer upwards of minerals through the soil horizons caused by evaporation loss at the surface.
Leaching	Downward washing by rainwater of soluble ions in solution.
Eluviation	The leaching of small suspended soil particles in infiltrating water from the A horizon.
Illuviation	The deposition of leached or eluvial particles into the B horizon.
Mor humus	Acid humus formed by the decaying of pine needles.
Mull humus	Soft, blackish organic matter formed by the decaying of deciduous leaves.

Factors determining soil type

Climate
- Temperature: determines the length of the growing season, the supply of organic material (amount of humus) and the speed of decomposition, which will be faster in warmer climates.
- Rainfall: where rainfall totals and intensity are high there will be more leaching and in areas of less rainfall more evaporation will lead to increased capillary action.

Organisms and vegetation
- Active micro-organisms will increase the amount of nitrogen fixation and the decomposition of dead vegetation, leading to an increased depth of humus.
- The type of vegetation determines the type of organic matter and therefore the pH. Most British soils are slightly acidic, particularly as heavy rainfall leaches out calcium, which is an alkali.

Relief

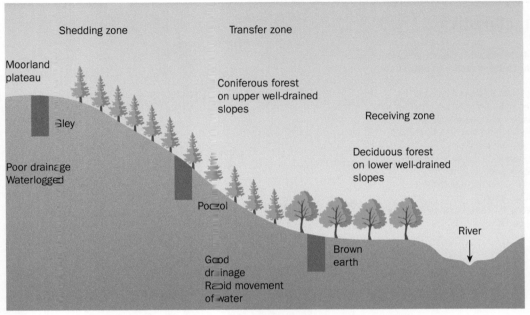

Diagram of a soil catena – this shows the relationship between soils and relief

Parent material

- This is the major factor determining soil type.
- It provides a supply of minerals and controls soil depth, texture, drainage (permeability) and soil quality.

Soil profiles and processes

For each soil type you need to think about its **characteristics** (what it looks like), **formation** (key factors as to why it became, e.g. a brown earth and not a podzol) and **processes** (what is going on within the soil profile).

Brown earth

Characteristics

- Precipitation exceeds evapotranspiration.
- This soil is associated with deciduous forest.
- Generally pH 5 (slightly acidic).
- Pedalfer soil – so rich in hydrogen.
- Litter layer decomposes rapidly.
- A horizon is not bleached as rainfall totals are moderate.
- Clay minerals have been washed down and redeposited in B horizon.
- The high clay content gives it a distinctive texture.
- Good soils for cereal crops and good for grazing cattle.

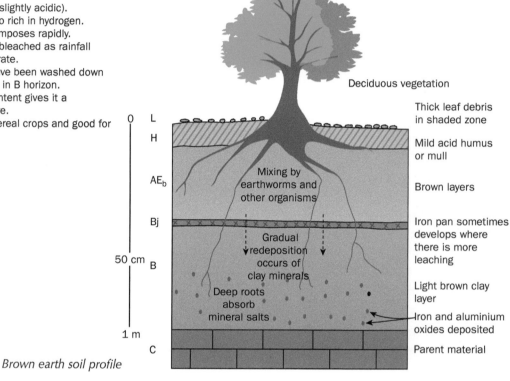

Deciduous vegetation

Thick leaf debris in shaded zone

Mild acid humus or mull

Brown layers

Iron pan sometimes develops where there is more leaching

Light brown clay layer

Iron and aluminium oxides deposited

Parent material

Mixing by earthworms and other organisms

Gradual redeposition occurs of clay minerals

Deep roots absorb mineral salts

0   L
     H
     AE_b
     Bj
50 cm B
1 m
     C

Brown earth soil profile

Formation

- Climate: temperate climates with moderate rainfall. Precipitation exceeds evapotranspiration.
- Vegetation: deciduous forests. Thick leaf litter layer that decomposes quickly.
- Organisms: active decomposers and worms, insects and rodents that help mix the soil.
- Relief: good drainage, possibly on a slope.
- Parent material: semi-permeable/permeable, good supply of minerals.

Processes

- Leaching, translocation.
- In the A horizon clay minerals are washed down and redeposited in the B horizon.
- In areas of less rainfall the clay may remain, and only soluble minerals like calcium will move down.
- Iron or hard pans (these are thin layers of redeposited iron and form an impermeable barrier between horizons) sometimes develop where there is more leaching. Leaching is the removal of soluble minerals such as nitrogen (N), magnesium (Mg) and calcium (Ca) from the surface layers of the soil by the downward movement of acidic rainwater. Conditions that favour leaching are: heavy rainfall, free-draining soil and acid humus.
- Human use: good soils for growing cereal crops and good grazing land for cattle.

Podzol

Characteristics

- Occur where precipitation exceeds evapotranopiration.
- Coniferous forest/heathland vegetation in northern hemisphere.
- Usually colder climate so organic matter decomposes slowly.
- Pine needles form a thin litter layer so the humus is very acidic which makes iron (Fe) and aluminium (Al) more soluble.
- Rainfall leaches the iron and aluminium from the A horizon leaving it a bleached ashy white.
- The iron is washed down into the Bf (iron pan) layer usually in winter.
- This hard, thin red or blackish iron pan layer is impermeable.
- This soil has limited agricultural potential but it can be improved by artificial drainage and the application of lime.
- Crops grown – oats, potatoes and hay.

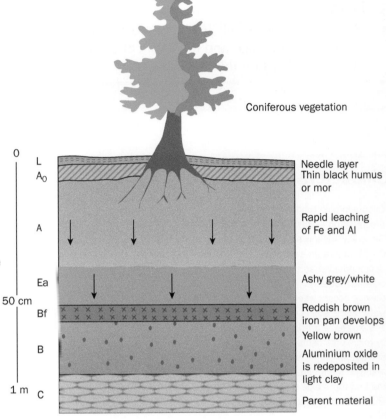

Podzol soil profile

Formation

- Climate: high northern latitudes with high rainfall and cool temperatures. Precipitation exceeds evapotranspiration.
- Vegetation: taiga, coniferous forest and/or heathland. Thin litter layer of pine needles so the humus layer is very acidic, which makes iron (Fe) and aluminium (Al) more soluble.
- Organisms: cool temperatures mean decomposition happens slowly or not at all.
- Relief: free drained upper slopes.
- Parent material: well-drained or sandy soils.

Processes

- Podzolization, eluviations, illuviation, leaching.
- Podzolization only takes place where you have an acid humus layer and intense leaching with acid rainwater passing through the A horizon and breaking down iron and aluminium oxide.
- Rainfall leaches iron and aluminium from the A horizon, leaving it a bleached ash-white colour.

- The iron is washed down (eluviated) in its blue (ferrous) conditon into (illuviated) the B horizon mainly in winter. As the soil dries in spring, oxygen can re-enter the soil and the iron oxidises to its red (ferric) state. The B horizon adopts an orange colour.
- The hard, thin red or blackish layer is iron rich and called the iron or hard pan. It is impermeable.
- Human use: these soils have limited agricultural potential but they can be improved by artificial drainage and the application of lime. Oats, potatoes and hay are the only cultivated crops on this soil type.

Gley

Characteristics

- Occurs in cold tundra areas with low precipitation and evapotranspiration.
- Generally shallow soils.
- Cold temperatures slow down decomposition so there is little organic matter.
- Gleying occurs when the output of water in the soil is restricted. The oxygen is quickly used up by micro-organisms and this deoxygenates the soil water and with the stagnant conditions the iron turns blue (ferrous).
- This leads to the soil being tinged blue or grey.
- However, mottled orange occurs whenever oxygen penetrates down the plant root channels or through cracks.
- A true gley is formed over a thick clay parent material.
- This type of soil can also form at the bottom of a slope or in a depression where drainage is poor.

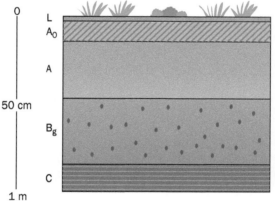

Gley soil profile

Formation

- Climate: temperate, tundra regions. Precipitation exceeds evapotranspiration. Cool to cold temperatures.
- Vegetation: grasses and low shrubs. Organic layer only partially decomposes.
- Organisms: few as too cold.
- Relief: poorly drained areas such as the bottom of a slope or in a depression. In tundra areas the permafrost means drainage is impeded.
- Parent material: usually thick clay and impermeable.

Processes

- Gleying.
- Oxygen depletion by bacteria in a stagnant waterlogged soil.
- This soil occurs when the output of water in the soil is restricted. The oxygen is quickly used up by micro-organisms and this deoxygenates the soil water and together with the stagnant conditions the iron turns blue (ferrous).
- This leads to the B horizon being tinged blue or grey.
- However, mottled orange occurs wherever oxygen has penetrated down a root channel or crack.
- Human use: these have very little economic potential.

This website has excellent photographs of the three soils along with details of their characteristics:
http://www.macaulay.ac.uk/soilquality/Soils%20 and%20their%20main%20characteristics.pdf

TOP TIP

Make sure you practice sketching and labelling all three soil profiles.

TOP TIP

Learn all the soil definitions carefully and be able to explain them in relation to all three soil types.

EXAM QUESTION

For a podzol, **explain** the main conditions and soil-forming processes that have led to its formation.

5 marks

Population

In this section

- methods and problems of data collection
- consequences of population structure
- causes and impacts of forced and voluntary migration

The growing world population

The world's population is growing fastest in the **developing** countries (e.g. Tanzania) and more slowly in the **developed** countries (e.g. United Kingdom). In countries like Japan the population is decreasing.

According to the UN, the world's population will reach 9 billion by 2050 and 10 billion by 2100.

Population growth is the difference between birth rate and death rate. These figures are usually measured using per thousand. The symbol for per thousand is ‰.

The global population reached 7 billion in 2011

Census – more than just a population count

Take a look at this news article on the 2011 census:
http://www.bbc.co.uk/news/uk-12873011

The census is a survey carried out in the UK every 10 years by the government to collect information on:

- **Demographic data:** number of people, age and gender.
- **Social data:** marital status, citizenship, ethnic group, religion, languages spoken and education.
- **Economic data:** occupation, income, unemployment, type of housing, car ownership and mode of transport used to get to work.

Advantages and disadvantages of doing a census

Advantages	Disadvantages
The government can forecast demographic change and plan ahead on how to best spend and save the country's tax revenue (health care, social services, education, pension, housing, transport and other infrastructure).	It is very expensive – the last census in 2011 cost the UK government £480 million. The cost of carrying out a census is too expensive for some developing countries.
Academics use the data to study the changes in society.	It takes at least two years to process the information – by that time the information is out of date.
Genealogists use old censuses to trace ancestry.	Result isn't 100% accurate – some people write false information or do not return their census at all.

Reasons for inaccuracies in developing countries

- **Size of the country:** some countries' territories are vast – for example India is 13 times bigger than the UK, which makes it very difficult to cover every part of the country.
- **The terrain:** mountainous countries like Nepal and Pakistan have poor or no roads to access the population in remote areas.
- **The climate:** some roads become impassable during hurricane/rainy season.
- **Nomadic population:** around 4% of Tanzania's population is considered to be nomadic (Maasai and Luo). Nomadic people move frequently as part of their traditional lifestyle, which makes it very difficult to get an accurate count of the population.
- **Literacy rate:** Afghanistan's literacy rate is only 28% which means the vast majority of the population is illiterate and therefore can't read the census questions and can't provide a written answer. The government will have to spend money on employing enumerators to conduct the census orally. People are less willing to give private information to enumerators, which leads to more inaccuracies.
- **Communication:** in some countries there are many languages spoken – India for example has more than 20 official languages, and in Papua New Guinea 820 different indigenous languages are spoken. Censuses will have to be translated, which adds to the cost, and some questions may not be translated well or accurately.
- **Lack of trust:** some countries have suffered major civil unrest (like Rwanda in 1994). This could mean people are less likely to trust the government and therefore less likely to answer the questions honestly.
- **Cost of carrying out the census:** most developing countries lack money and other resources to do a census every 10 years. They also lack the technology to process the information efficiently.
- **Inflated numbers:** community leaders may encourage the local population to write inflated population numbers in the hope of getting more funding for services from the central government.

- **Exceptional events:** in the summer of 2014 much of West Africa was under threat from the Ebola virus. Sierra Leone was scheduled to hold a census in December 2014 but this has now been postponed until at least December 2015. While epidemics can happen anywhere in the world, developing countries find it harder to control the diseases due to lack of resources.
- **Current civil unrest:** Syria was scheduled to hold a census in 2014, but this has been delayed until at least November 2015.

Case study of a developing country: Nigeria

Nigeria is often referred to as the 'Giant of Africa' as it is the most populous country on the continent and the 7th most populous in the world. The Nigerian government find it challenging to collect accurate population data because of the following complex factors:

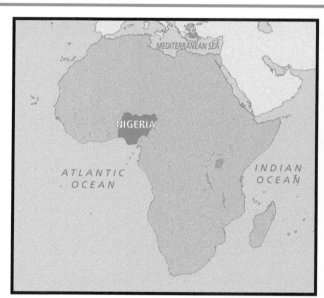

Nigeria in the continent of Africa

- Nigeria is twice the size of the UK. This makes it difficult to reach everyone in the country.

- Nigeria's roads and railways are poorly maintained. Some rural settlements are very difficult to reach, especially in the rainy season when roads become impassable.

- Nigeria's border with Cameroon has a sizeable mountain range called the Atlantika Mountains, which is remote and not easily accessible.

- Nigeria is home to over 18 million nomadic tribespeople, known as Fulani (who make up around 10% of the population). They make a living from herding cattle, goats and sheep. The majority of the Fulani migrate around West Africa in search of grazing ground for their animals. North of Nigeria is also home to another nomadic tribe called the Tuareg. Nomadic people usually do not have a fixed settlement and they move around West Africa throughout the year, making them difficult to count.

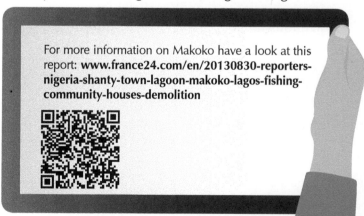

For more information on Makoko have a look at this report: **www.france24.com/en/20130830-reporters-nigeria-shanty-town-lagoon-makoko-lagos-fishing-community-houses-demolition**

- Lagos is Nigeria's largest city. There are approximately 100,000 people in Lagos who live in a shanty town called Makoko. The shanty town population is growing rapidly due to rural–urban migration. To count people in the shanty town is a difficult task because the residents do not have a proper address which the census form can be sent to, or an enumerator can visit. Due to the recent threat of eviction from the mayor of Lagos, people in the shanty town distrust the local government and are therefore less willing to answer questions.

- Although the 'official' language of Nigeria is English, there are 500 other languages and dialects spoken in Nigeria. This makes it difficult and costly to translate the census questions. Due to limitations with literal translation, certain words can be mistranslated between languages and this can lead to inaccuracy.

- Only 61% of Nigerians are literate. This means the government will have to employ larger numbers of enumerators to go around each settlement to ask questions in person. This is time consuming and expensive.

- Even in a modern democratic country, Nigeria's politics is divided down tribal lines. People from a certain village or tribe may give inflated numbers for their population in order to obtain more resources from the central government or to increase political representation.

- Three northern states in Nigeria have been attacked by a terrorist group called 'Boko Haram'. The civil unrest has led to displacement of 250,000 people and a further 3 million people are facing a humanitarian crisis. In such a politically unstable environment it will be very difficult to obtain accurate data as people may feel frightened to answer ethnic or religious questions one way or another.

- Even once the census data is collected, developing countries like Nigeria lack the resources and statistical experts to process such a large volume of data into useable information, which defeats the purpose of carrying out a census in the first place

- Nigeria's last census in 2006 is largely seen as an inaccurate count by population experts.

You can read more about the Nigerian census here: **http://news.bbc.co.uk/1/hi/world/ africa/4512240.stm** and **http://allafrica.com/ stories/201407290316.html**

Other ways to collect demographic data

Civil register

Most countries have a civil register: birth, marriage and death certificates (also known as **vital statistics**) are legal documents. In Scotland, births, marriages and deaths need to be registered within 21 days of the event.

Government departments

The UK and Scottish government statistical departments are:

- Office for National Statistics and UK Statistics Authority are responsible for collecting and publishing statistics related to the economy, population and society at national, regional and local levels.

- Scottish Neighbourhood Statistics is the Scottish Government's on-going programme to improve the availability, consistency and accessibility of statistics in Scotland.

- Since 2004, the UK government has collected additional population data by conducting an annual population survey. This is a survey carried out on a small random sample of people (360,000 individuals). Its purpose is to provide information on key social and socio-economic variables between the 10-yearly censuses, with particular emphasis on providing information relating to sub-regional (local authority) areas.

Organised research

There are also research organizations that deal with population statistics:

- YouGov is an online-based research company that collects data and people's opinions about current affairs. Public organisations and private companies often use the findings of YouGov to make decisions about goods and services.

- The Institute of Public Policy Research (IPPR)'s purpose is to conduct and publish research into, and promote public education in the economic, social and political sciences, and in science and technology; including the effect of moral, social, political and scientific factors on public policy and on the living standards of all sections of the community.

Loyalty cards

Information about our shopping habits can be used to compile economic data.

Immigration

- Passport control at ports provides a record of the number of people coming into the country. When entering the United Kingdom, non-EU nationals are required to fill in a **landing card** providing a few basic pieces of information.

- Police registration is required for some nationalities as part of their visa condition.

European and global bodies

Eurostat collects European Union-wide data on economics, population, trade, industry and agriculture. The UN Statistical Division collects world-wide data on social, economic and environmental issues.

EXAM QUESTION

Nigeria conducted a population census in 2006. However, the chairperson of the National Population Commission stated in 2012 that 'Nigeria has no data. People can't really tell you precisely what the population is'. Another census will be conducted in 2016.

Explain the problems of collecting accurate population data in developing countries.

6 marks

Population data presentation

Two of the most useful ways to show population structure and change are the demographic transition model (line graph) and the population pyramid (bar graph).

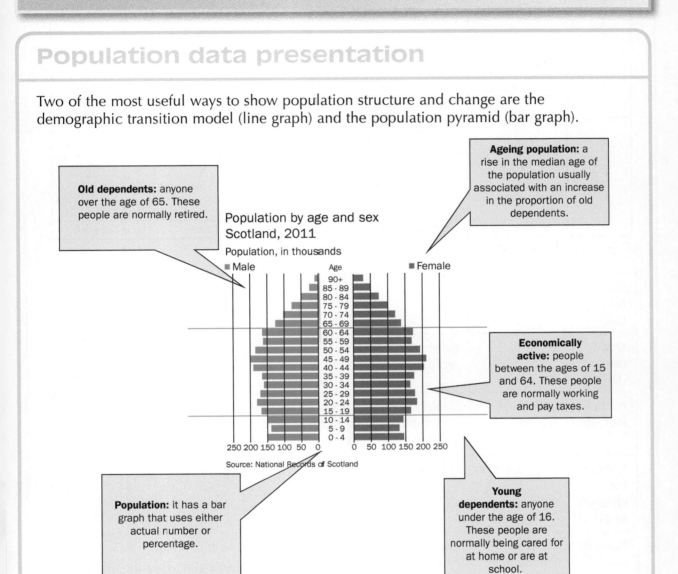

Ageing population: a rise in the median age of the population usually associated with an increase in the proportion of old dependents.

Old dependents: anyone over the age of 65. These people are normally retired.

Economically active: people between the ages of 15 and 64. These people are normally working and pay taxes.

Population: it has a bar graph that uses either actual number or percentage.

Young dependents: anyone under the age of 16. These people are normally being cared for at home or are at school.

Population pyramid

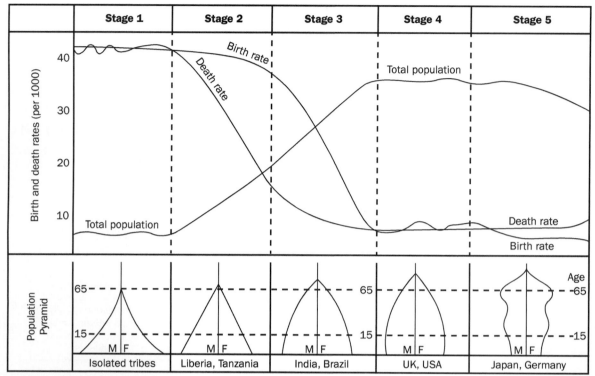

Demographic transition model

	Stage 1	Stage 2	Stage 3	Stage 4	Stage 5
Birth rate (BR)	High	High	Falling	Low	Very low
Death rate (DR)	High	Falling rapidly	Continues to fall	Low	Low
Natural increase	Very little / stable	Rapid / very rapid increase	Continues to increase at slower rate	Slow increase / stable	Slow Starts to decrease
Reasons for changes in BR	See case study of Tanzania		Improvement and development	See case study of Japan	
Reasons for changes in DR	Diseases, famine. Poor medical knowledge and access, resulting in high infant mortality and low life expectancy.	Improvement in medical care and access to care. Cleaner water supply and better provision of sanitation.		Good health care. Good standard of living and quality of life.	

Consequences of population structure

Case study of an ageing population: Japan

Japan is at stage 5 of the demographic transition model (DTM) and it is the fastest ageing country in the world; the baby boomer generation (people born 1947–49) have reached retirement age.

Japan's birth rate is lower than its death rate – this means the population is ageing and declining. For the last 30 years the number of babies born in Japan has been decreasing.

You can read more about Japan's falling birth rate here: **http://www.bbc.co.uk/news/world-asia-30653825**

Japan: Population Data	
Population	127.3 million
Birth rate	8‰
Death rate	10‰
Natural increase	−0.2%
Life expectancy	83 years
% of population age 15 and under	13%
% of population age 65 and over	25%
Fertility rate per woman	1.4
% of urban population	92%
GNI per capita	US$ 46,140
DTM stage	Stage 5

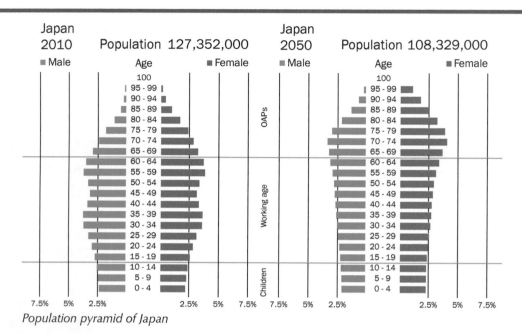

Population pyramid of Japan

Japan's birth rate is at an all-time low because:

- Women are choosing to give birth later and have fewer offspring so they can pursue their ambitions, e.g. for further education and having a career.

- In most developing countries children are seen as economic burdens as it is very expensive to raise a family. Japan is one of the most expensive places to buy a house, and most people cannot afford to buy their own house so they rent throughout their lives.

- Although education is free it is very competitive to get into prestigious universities so parents have to spend a lot of money on extra tuition and extra-curricular activities.

- Japan's maternity leave is only 14 weeks and during this time the new mothers are paid 67% of their normal pay. Job security for new mothers is not 100% and they are less likely to be promoted later in their careers.

Some consequences of the low birth rate are:

- The population of Japan is decreasing. It is estimated that in the next 50 years the country's population will shrink by a third.

- Fewer babies being born means less money needs to be spent on pre- and post-natal care. Some maternity hospitals will close and some midwives will lose their jobs.

- Fewer children also means less money needs to be spent on childcare and education. This will lead to some schools amalgamating or closing and some teachers will lose their jobs.

- Redundant doctors, nurses and teachers will have to be paid unemployment benefits and they may also need to be retrained for other professions. This is very expensive for the government.

- In the long term companies will find it difficult to recruit young workers.

- The profits of companies producing goods and services for babies and children may suffer.

Due to a healthy diet, lifestyle and good health service, Japan's life expectancy is one of the highest in the world. In 2013 Japanese people aged 65 or older were at a record high, making up a quarter of the population.

Consequences of an ageing population are:

- A low fertility rate means a lower number of economically-active members of the population. This means fewer working-age people will have to support a larger ageing population, meaning the government will have to raise taxes.

- Old people are more likely to be ill and require medical care. More resources will need to be spent on geriatric services. Old people also require more assistance with day-to-day tasks, so more nursing homes and day care centres will have to be built.

- A smaller economically-active population means Japan's economy will suffer from a lack of skilled workers, making the country less competitive in the global market.

- Until recently the mandatory retirement age in Japan was 60 but the government has raised this to 65.

- Older people are encouraged to stay on working after their official retirement age at reduced hours and responsibility. There has been a significant increase in the 'silver workforce' in Japan. Older workers are valued for their maturity and experience.

- As a result of its decreasing population Japan will most likely relax its strict immigration rules to let more immigrants live and work in Japan.

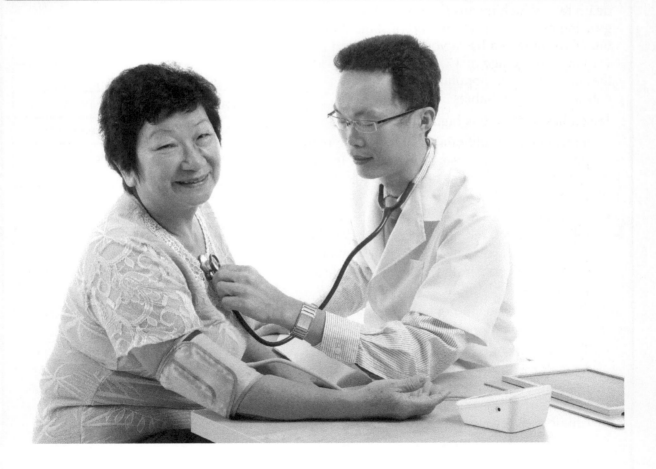

Case study of a rapidly growing population: Tanzania

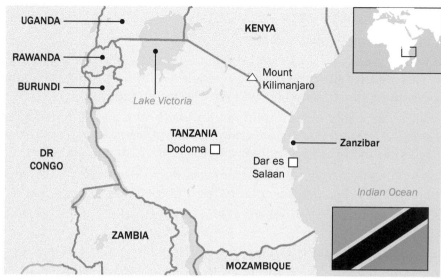

Map showing the location of Tanzania

Tanzania is a developing country located in East Africa. It has a high birth rate and a low death rate, which means the population is growing rapidly: it is at the end of stage 2 of the DTM. Tanzania has a young population with an average age of 17. This means that the majority of the population is yet to get married and have babies.

Tanzania's birth rate is high because:

- Tanzania is a traditional country where many people still hold conservative values. In such societies large families are considered to be normal.

- Many people in Tanzania hold conservative religious values and it is largely considered to be taboo to have an abortion. Approximately 10 million people in Tanzania are Catholics.

- In developing countries it is more difficult and costly to obtain contraception and advice on family planning.

- Tanzania's economy is heavily based on agriculture. In rural communities 85% of the population is engaged in farming. In traditional rural communities children are seen as economic assets, as they can work and help on the farm from a relatively young age. Children in Tanzania also take on their share of the domestic duties and some go out to work from a young age to supplement the family income.

- Tanzania doesn't have a state pension for everyone so parents will have more children to make sure someone will look after them in their old age.

Tanzania: Population Data	
Population	49.3 million
Birth rate	40‰
Death rate	9‰
Natural increase	3%
Life expectancy	61 years
% of population age 15 and under	45%
% of population age 65 and over	3%
Fertility rate per woman	5.3
% of urban population	28%
GNI per capita	US$ 630
DTM stage	End of stage 2

- The female literacy rate in Tanzania is 67%, which means one third of the female population cannot read and write. Illiterate girls go on to marry early and produce a large number of children. On average a Tanzanian woman will give birth to 5–6 children in her lifetime.
- Due to poverty and lack of education, infectious diseases such as malaria and cholera kill a lot of newborns. The infant mortality rate in Tanzania is high (45%). Parents have lots of children to compensate for the high infant mortality rate.

The consequences of a rapidly growing population are:

- Overcrowding in urbanised areas due to the large number of young people in search of a job. This leads to the growth of shanty towns and informal settlements.
- Unemployment or underemployment may be high due to a large workforce and not enough jobs.
- The government needs to build more schools and hospitals. The Tanzanian government do not have the money to build enough facilities, so people suffer from poor services.
- More teachers need to be trained in order for everyone to obtain a decent quality of education.
- The government must work hard to attract investment from national and international companies to create more jobs. The government will continue to receive foreign aid to fund the programmes needed to develop the country.

Migration

Reasons for moving away from a person's original location are called **push factors,** and reasons to move to another location are called **pull factors**.

Common push and pull factors

Push factors	Pull factors
Unemployment	Potential for employment
Lack of safety	A safer atmosphere
Lack of services	Better service provision
Poverty	Greater wealth
Crop failure	Fertile land
Drought	Good food supplies
War, civil unrest	Political security
Hazards	Less risk of natural hazards
Isolation	Friends and family

Migration can happen within the same country; this is known as **internal migration**. Migration can also be between two different countries and this is known as **international migration**.

Causes and impact of voluntary migration

Case study: Poland to Scotland

Characteristics

* Poland and Scotland have close historical ties.
* Today people born in Poland constitute the largest non-UK-born group in Scotland. It is estimated that 56,000 residents of Scotland were born in Poland.
* In 2004 Poland joined the European Union and since then the number of Polish-born residents in Scotland has increased due to ease of movement and right to employment.

Migration from Poland to Scotland

Incentives to move

Push factors:

* Lack of jobs – in 2004 the average unemployment rate in Poland was 18.9%. Unemployment in rural areas was as high as 40%.
* Lower wages at around £3 per hour average.

- Lower gross domestic product (GDP) per capita. GDP of Poland is $13648/capita and GDP of UK is $41787/capita.

Pull factors:

- Scotland was experiencing a skills shortage and needed more workers to fill vacancies in factories, farms, the service industry and in construction.
- Higher wages at on average £6 per hour, but depending on the type of jobs some workers were earning five times more than they would back in Poland.
- Plenty of low-cost flights are in operation between Poland and the UK.

Positive impact on Poland (donor country):

- Unemployment rate has fallen to 9%.
- Approximately £1.2 billion is sent from the UK to relatives in Poland every year (remittances), which helps them and the local economy.
- When Polish immigrants decided to return home they can speak English; this makes them more desirable to employers in Poland.

Negative impact on Poland (donor country):

- The majority of emigrants are of working age, leaving some settlements where the majority of people left are children and old people.
- More males emigrate than females, resulting in a gender imbalance.
- Lots of highly educated and well-qualified people left Poland – this is referred to as a **brain drain** and leaves fewer working age and well-qualified people in the donor country.

Positive impact on Scotland (host country):

- Polish is the second most commonly used language in Scotland and in the UK.
- Enriches the cultural diversity of Scotland.
- Increases the working population and reduces labour shortages.
- Polish immigrants are more willing to take on lower paid jobs, which may have unsociable working hours (service sector) or difficult working conditions (processing and manufacturing jobs). Scottish companies who employ Polish workers will benefit from a lower wage bill, making the company more competitive and their products/services better value for consumers.

Negative impact on Scotland (host country):

- Overcrowding in schools due to sudden increase in the roll.
- Money and resources needed for extra English literacy classes at school and also in the community for the adult population.
- Some GP surgeries and hospitals initially found it difficult to understand the Polish patients due to the language barrier.
- Overcrowding in the affordable parts of the city. Strain on the local housing stock.
- Language barriers may lead to misunderstanding, mistrust and friction between the Polish people and the local communities.
- During an economic downturn, Polish immigrants may become the target of frustration caused by higher unemployment rates.
- Immigrants are often blamed for 'undercutting' wages as they are willing to work for lower wages and often for longer hours.

Causes and impacts of forced migration

Case study: Syria

Characteristics

Much of the Middle East, including Syria, has been politically unstable since the so-called Arab Spring in 2010, when a series of protests, riots and civil wars broke out in many Arab countries.

Syria has been in a state of civil war since March 2011. Over 200,000 people have died as a result of the fighting between the Syrian government and the rebel groups.

Syrian city of Homs destroyed by civil war

According to UNHCR (United Nations High Commissioner for Refugees) 3.7 million people have fled Syria since the start of the conflict. Syrians first fled in vast numbers to neighbouring Lebanon, Turkey and Jordan. In addition, 6.5 million people are internally displaced, in search for a safe place to live.

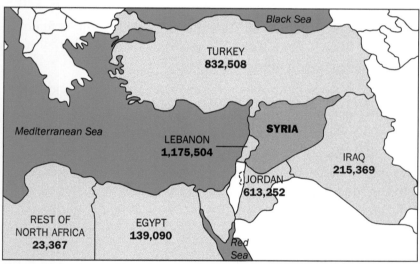

Estimated number and location of Syrian refugees, UNHCR

Incentives to move

Push factors:

- Thousands of Syrians flee their country every day. They often decide to finally escape after seeing their neighbourhoods bombed or family members killed.
- Bombings are destroying crowded cities.
- Horrific human rights violations are widespread.
- Thousands of people have been killed, kidnapped, tortured and raped.
- Basic necessities like food and medical care are sparse.
- Over 4 million people have been left homeless.
- Much of the country's infrastructure and essential services have been destroyed.

- Thousands of people are unemployed.
- For many Syrians it is impossible to lead a normal life.

Pull factors:

- Many Syrians have family and friends already living abroad so it is easier to make the move.
- Syria has porous land borders with Turkey, Lebanon and Jordan which makes it relatively easy to migrate into these countries, even without a passport.

Impact on donor country (Syria):

- Much of Syria's educated elite population (those who have money and connections) have fled their home in search of safety.
- Syria does not have enough doctors and nurses to look after the injured and the weak.
- Once vibrant cities such as Homs and Aleppo are now ghost towns.

Impact on host countries (Lebanon, Turkey and Jordan) – now home to over 3 million Syrian refugees

- The majority of Syrian refugees are living in Jordan and Lebanon. In the region's two smallest countries, weak infrastructure and limited resources are nearing breaking point under the strain.
- In some towns the population has doubled, putting a lot of pressure on health and education services.
- Waste management is not coping. Space is also an issue in crowded urban centres, rents in some places have trippled since the influx of refugees.
- There are not enough teachers. Some schools send Lebanese children home at lunchtime and then teach Syrian children for the second half of the day.
- Some Lebanese people say they have lost their jobs because Syrians are willing to work for less, or that they have been evicted because Syrians share housing with many people, and can therefore afford rents that the Lebanese cannot.
- Since August 2014 more Syrians have escaped into northern Iraq at a newly opened border crossing. In a country that is still recovering from its own prolonged conflict this influx is dramatic and brings additional challenges.
- An increasing number of Syrian refugees are fleeing across the border into Turkey, overwhelming urban host communities and creating new cultural tensions and resentments.

EXAM QUESTION

2012 saw a significant increase in Germany's population. This was not due to a sudden baby boom, but to the many immigrants moving to the country. Experts point out this could result in both benefits and problems.

Referring to a named case study, **analyse** the impact of migration on either the donor country or the host country.

5 marks

Rural

Rural land degradation in North Africa

North Africa – the Sahel region

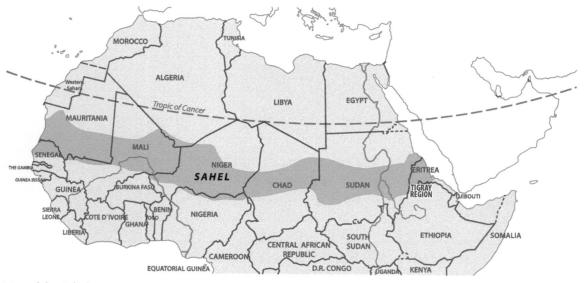

Map of the Sahel

The Sahel is a narrow band of land that stretches across North Africa. It is a semi-arid area that borders the southern edge of the Sahara. Many of the countries, e.g. Sudan, Eritrea, northern Ethiopia, in this region are susceptible to the process of desertification. This is the degradation of soil and vegetation cover and can occur in any of the dry areas of the world, not just desert fringes. 30% of the world's surface is under threat of desertification.

Desertification is defined as 'the spread of desert-like conditions in an arid or semi-arid area due to climate change or human influence'.

Physical causes of desertification

Unreliable rainfall and drought: in the Sahel rainfall is confined to just a few months in the northern hemisphere's 'summer', due to the arrival of the ITCZ. However, the total annual mean rainfall and the length of the wet season are both very unreliable. Periods of drought since the late 1960s are now more common as can be seen from the graph on the following page and this may be due to the ITCZ not migrating as far north in these years. It is thought this could be due to climate change.

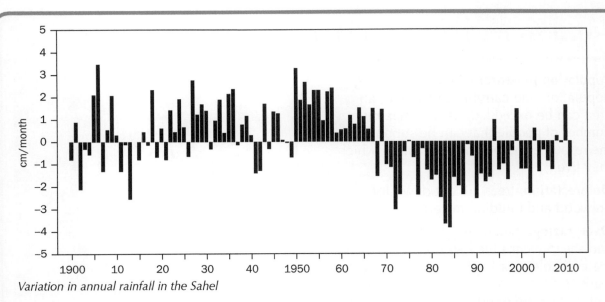

Variation in annual rainfall in the Sahel

Lowering of the water table: through prolonged drought and water abstraction from wells. This means certain plant roots can no longer reach a water supply.

Flash flooding: the rain often falls in a few heavy downpours and most is lost as surface runoff with very little infiltrating into the ground.

Water erosion: topsoil is washed away by the impact of raindrops (rainsplash), sheets of water (sheet wash), small surface streams that erode channels and deep gulleys (rill and gully erosion) that carve up the landscape.

Wind erosion: strong winds lift soil particles and blow them for up to several kilometres, creating dust storms. They are moved in three different ways:

- **Suspension**: very fine material (<0.15mm) is picked up and carried large distances by the wind.

- **Saltation**: fine and coarse grain sand particles are lifted first vertically and then they are bounced in a leap-frogging action over each other.

- **Surface creep**: small stones and pebbles are dislodged by the moving sand grains and are rolled along the land surface.

Human causes of desertification

Population pressure: with an increasing population, the carrying capacity of an area can be exceeded, i.e. the maximum number of people that can be supported by the resources of the environment in which they live.

Deforestation: trees are cut down for firewood and building materials.

Overgrazing: the grazing of too many goats and sheep means the carrying capacity of the available grassland is exceeded and this leads to surface vegetation being stripped with little hope of it being re-established.

Children living in the Sahel region

Overcultivation: growing crops on the same areas of land for years without giving it a rest. This leads to a breakdown in soil structure, fertility and makes the land more susceptible to soil erosion.

Monoculture farming: growing the same crop for many years, which depletes the soil of moisture and nutrients.

Poor irrigation practices: farmers applying large amounts of water to their fields causes salts to leach out of the soil as it encourages the process of capillary action – salts in solution are transported through the soil horizons to the soil surface. Eventually this leads to soils that are uncultivable.

Cultivation of marginal land: fragile land that should not be used for crop growing.

Increased water extraction: with little or no surface water stores more wells have to be sunk to tap into groundwater sources and this contributes to the lowering water table.

Consequences of desertification

Social	Economic	Environmental
Decrease in human wellbeing, e.g. poverty, famine, malnutrition.	Loss of crop production/ yield.	Decrease in vegetation cover – pasture dries up.
Traditional nomadic way of life in Sahel areas is under threat.	Decline in biological productivity, e.g. growth of trees.	Increased soil salinity due to poor irrigation methods.
Increased rural–urban migration from areas suffering from desertification, particularly to towns and cities.	Animals, e.g. goats, sheep, cattle die due to starvation.	Increased dust storm frequency.

Social	Economic	Environmental
Families turn to 'famine foods', e.g. leaves in times of food shortages; these are nutritionally poor.	Stops development.	Increased surface albedo – this is the reflectiveness of a surface; with loss of vegetation albedo increases as more incoming solar radiation is reflected back into the atmosphere.
Wells dry up – through over abstraction of water.		Decrease in biomass (amount of organic matter from living vegetation, i.e. leaf fall).
Political instability as a result of different 'tribes' coming together in urban areas.		Decrease in soil organic matter.
		Loss of key plant species.
		Loss of key animal species.

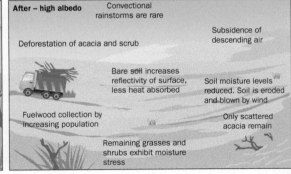

Effects of changing albedo on the landscape

TOP TIP

Just as in the River basin management topic you should be able to divide the consequences of desertification into social, economic and environmental consequences.

Possible solutions to desertfication

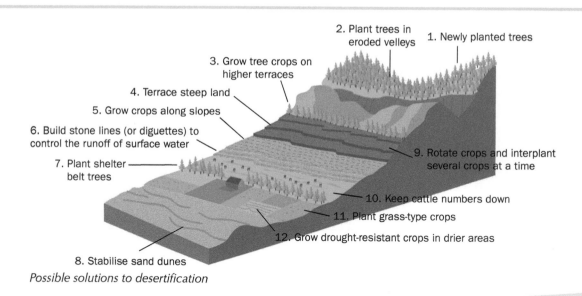

2. Plant trees in eroded velleys

1. Newly planted trees

3. Grow tree crops on higher terraces

4. Terrace steep land

5. Grow crops along slopes

6. Build stone lines (or diguettes) to control the runoff of surface water

7. Plant shelter belt trees

9. Rotate crops and interplant several crops at a time

10. Keep cattle numbers down

11. Plant grass-type crops

12. Grow drought-resistant crops in drier areas

8. Stabilise sand dunes

Possible solutions to desertification

Researchers have concluded that some of the most severe cases of land degradation in semi-arid areas could be reversed with the right policies and actions.

TOP TIP

Make sure you know all the physical and human causes of desertification and a number of solutions, and can explain them.

Case study: Tigray, Ethiopia

In regions like Tigray in northern Ethiopia, Africa, which is part of the western Sahel region, rural land degradation has been a major problem. It is an area of highland with a population that has increased tenfold since the end of the civil war and a population density of 100 people per sq km. The majority of the population are subsistence farmers and over the years the land has become badly degraded. Land degradation here is the result of population pressure, frequent droughts and poor farming practices. Torrential summer rains cause soil erosion as topsoil is washed off the steep slopes. However, local people are gradually beginning to coax it back to recovery with help from experts.

Watch the video 'Regreening Ethiopia's Highlands: A New Hope for Africa' at **http://www.youtube. com/watch?v=nak-UUZnvPl**

Some of the management practices introduced include:

- The government terraced steep slopes and built stone bunds. These are stone walls that follow the contours of the hills and they prevent soil erosion and flooding.
- Grazing animals, e.g. goats are kept in enclosed areas near settlements and fodder is brought to them rather than letting them graze on open ground.
- Areas of extreme degradation were closed off to grazing, crop cultivation and tree felling.
- Forests were replanted.

Since these management practices were introduced in the 1980s there has been a 'remarkable recovery of vegetation and also improved soil protection'.

Although the government initiated the recovery, local communities came to recognise the value of such conservation work because they could see the benefits, such as reduced flooding and less soil loss.

EXAM QUESTIONS

1. a) Explain the purpose of building stone lines or bunds (or diguettes) as a strategy to stop land degradation in semi-arid areas.

b) Discuss the effectiveness of another strategy, referring to a case study of your choice.

6 marks

2. Discuss the social consequences of rural land degradation in a semi-arid area.

5 marks

Urban

The urban population

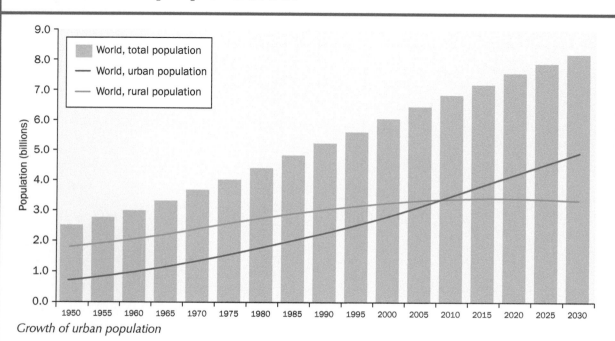

Growth of urban population

Urbanisation is the growth of towns and cities. In 2008, for the first time in human history, more people lived in the cities than in the countryside.

The status of 'megacity' is given to a settlement that has a population of 10 million and above. In 1975 there were three megacities (Tokyo, New Mexico and New York), now there are 30 and most of them are in developing counties. General population and urban population are both growing most rapidly in the economically less developed countries (ELDCs) and less so in the economically more developed countries (EMDCs).

All cities suffer from similar problems: pollution, traffic congestion, house price fluctuations, crime, demand for key services, demand for jobs, derelict land and urban decline.

TOP TIP

A very good television programme on this topic is Andrew Marr's 'Megacities' – you might be able to watch clips online.

Urban change and management in a developed world city: Glasgow

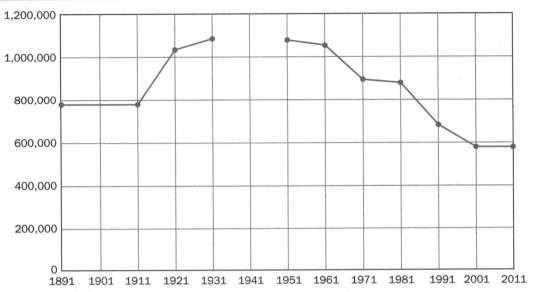

Population of Glasgow: census data

- Glasgow's population grew rapidly during the 19th and 20th centuries.
- New immigrants to Glasgow came from the Highlands and Islands of Scotland (early 1800s). This was followed by immigration of Irish (1840s), Italian (1890s), Jewish (WWII), Indian and Pakistani (1940s) and Polish (2000s) people.
- People came to Glasgow in search of jobs and to make a living in the city's booming industries.
- Most new immigrants settled in the inner city where rent was most affordable.
- The population of Glasgow peaked in the 1950s at 1.089 million.

TOP TIP

In an exam, name your case study city/area clearly at the beginning of your answer. Make sure your answer is detailed and not generic.

Changes to housing

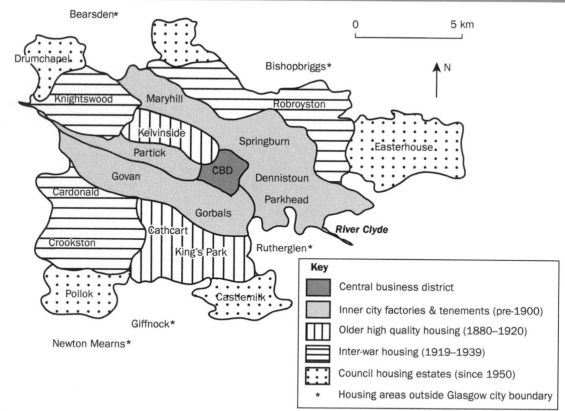

Inner city areas of Glasgow

Housing change in the Gorbals area of Glasgow was necessary because:

- By the 1930s the Gorbals had a reputation as the 'slum of Europe'.
- There was serious overcrowding.
- Lack of sanitation – no indoor bathrooms in tenements.
- Poor state of repair.
- Poor living conditions lead to poor health – Glasgow had the highest mortality rate from tuberculosis (TB) in Europe.

Changes were made in the 1960s by knocking down old tenements and building new **high rise flats**. These initially provided good accommodation but due to poor maintenance they were also demolished by the 1990s.

Construction of the high rise flats

Most recent changes to housing: 'New Gorbals'

- New Gorbals has a mixture of private and social housing.
- Some old tenements were kept. Instead of demolition they were renovated to modern standards.
- New houses are mid-rise with 3–4 floors, containing 6–8 units of flats with each flat having two or three bedrooms.
- Larger 'town house' properties have been built to encourage families to stay in New Gorbals.
- The area is well served by NHS services, schools and public transport. It also has a library, sports centre and shops.
- Old industrial sites have been decontaminated and cleared. The land was then used to build houses, offices and parks.

New flats on Thistle Terrace, New Gorbals

Changes to transport in Glasgow

There are many causes of traffic congestion, including:

Old and narrow streets

- Merchant City is the oldest part of the city and was built before the invention of cars so the streets are narrow. This problem is made worse by cars parking on the sides of the streets.
- There are many old historical buildings in Glasgow that cannot be knocked down to make wider streets.
- Streets close to George Square were laid out quickly during the Georgian period in a grid-iron pattern. This means traffic cannot flow smoothly due to there being many intersections in a relatively short space of time.

More cars on the road

- 69% of households in Scotland had at least one car or van in 2011 compared with 66% in 2001. In Glasgow at least 160,000 residents own a car.

Daily commute

- 49% of Glaswegians commute to work by car. The majority of people who work in the city centre do not live in the city – this creates morning and evening rush hours.

Effects of traffic congestion

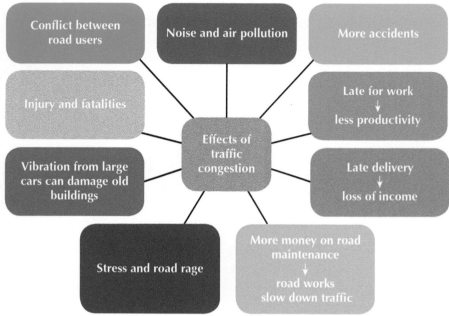

Effects of traffic congestion

Solutions to traffic congestion

Solutions	Effective?
One-way streets such as Hope Street and St Vincent Street.	Yes – traffic can move more smoothly **but** one-way systems can be confusing for drivers and it can take longer to reach your destination.
Motorway extension, e.g. M74 extension.	Yes – **but** it encourages more cars on the road which leads to more pollution.
More traffic wardens, parking meters, build more multi-storey car parks.	Yes – it discourages people from parking illegally which improves traffic flow. Parking fees can be expensive.
Build more bridges and tunnels and more footbridges (such as the 'squinty' and 'squiggly' bridges).	Yes – more bridge points between Southside of the city and the CBD will reduce congestion – more people now walk and cycle.
Improve public transport, Park and Ride systems, pedestrianise some streets.	Bus and cycle lanes make journeys on public transport quicker and people feel safer walking in CBD.

Solutions and effectiveness

EXAM QUESTION

For Glasgow, or any named developed world city you have studied, **explain** schemes that have been introduced to reduce problems of traffic management.

6 marks

Urban change and management in a developing world city: Kibera, Nairobi, Kenya

Nairobi is the capital city of Kenya, and is a city with a population of approximately 3.4 million people. The population of Nairobi has grown rapidly since the 1950s. 25% of Kenyans and 43% of the country's urban workers live in Nairobi.

Up to 60% of the total population of Nairobi lives in informal settlements known as shanty towns/slums. Kibera is one of the largest slums in Africa.

Need for management in Kibera

- Population of approximately 1 million.

- Massively overcrowded – the population density is 49,228/km².

- Average income is less than £1 a day, meaning over 50% of the population is living below the poverty line.

- Most people don't have a regular job. Two-thirds of the population work in the informal sector (black market).

- Up to 50% unemployment rate.

- Land is owned by the Kenyan government.

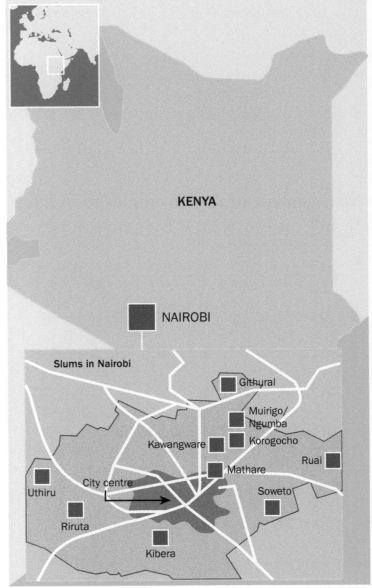

Map of Kenya highlighting the Nairobi slums

- Rent for a small tin shack is approximately £6 per month. 90% of the population are tenants with very little tenant security.
- 22% of the slum households have a water connection. There are two main water pipelines in the area and residents pay to collect water.
- No flushing toilets. One latrine is shared by 50–60 households.
- 20% of the population have electricity.
- No government-run clinics or hospitals.
- High crime rate.
- High number of street children and orphans.
- Many social problems related to drugs and alcohol.
- Very little help from the Kenyan government and Nairobi city council. Local officials and police force are often accused of being either uninterested in the slum problems or corrupt.
- There are no organised refuse collections. The land and water is heavily polluted.
- There is a lot of air pollution from the use of kerosene lamps and stoves due to lack of affordable electricity supply.
- High infant and child mortality rates, low life expectancy rate and recurring health problems: diarrhoea, malaria, TB.
- 60% of adult population are HIV positive.
- Low school enrolment and secondary school completion, especially for girls.

Management strategies employed in Kibera

- Slum upgrades by KENSUP (Kenya Slum Upgrading Programme).
- Micro-financing – a community-based financial service to help entrepreneurs start up businesses. Due to lack of official financial history normal banks are unwilling to lend to people from the slums. Micro-financing companies like KIVA will lend the money to help people help themselves out of poverty.
- Rain water collection.
- Peepoo bag – a personal, single-use, self-sanitising, fully biodegradable toilet that prevents faeces from contaminating the immediate area as well as the surrounding ecosystem. After use, Peepoo turns into valuable fertiliser that can improve livelihoods and increase food security.
- 'Adopt a Light' campaign by public–private partnership.
- Privatisation of some services like water distribution and refuse collection.
- Better arrangement of routes taken by minibus – same solutions for traffic congestion.
- Raising awareness and special campaigns.

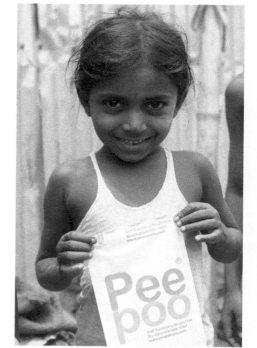

Child with 'Peepoo' bag – self-sanitising toilet

GOT IT? ☐ ☐ ☐

- Educating the public about the Citizens' Rights Charter – to empower the slum residents and give them the tools to make effective demands on the city council.
- City council's budgets and accounts are now published to increase transparency.
- Involvement of charities, non-governmental organisations (NGOs) and community-based organisations to help improve aspects of life in Kibera, e.g. Water Aid for sanitation programmes.
- The Scoring Goals project. This project gives children and young adults the opportunity to play in organised football games and participate in drama competitions, building confidence and self-esteem.

Limitations of the management strategies

- Nairobi city council is understaffed and under-resourced to deal with the slum problems.
- Poor resource management and accounting.
- Weak and inefficient revenue collection (tax) by the government and city council.
- Lack of communication and dialogue between the residents and the city council.

Here is a link to an informative documentary about Kibera: **http://youtu.be/jQeKEGrDoQ4**

EXAM QUESTION

With reference to a named city in a developing country, **discuss** the social, economic and environmental problems often found in such cities.

6 marks

River basin management

Global water surplus and deficiency

Management of the world's water resources is necessary as the hydrological cycle does not spread freshwater evenly over the globe. Some places have a surplus of water and other places have a water scarcity.

71% of the Earth's surface is water with 97% of that being salty and only 3% being fresh. Of this 3%, 2.25% is stored in ice caps and glaciers. This leaves only 0.75% of the Earth's water to be shared out amongst the world's growing population.

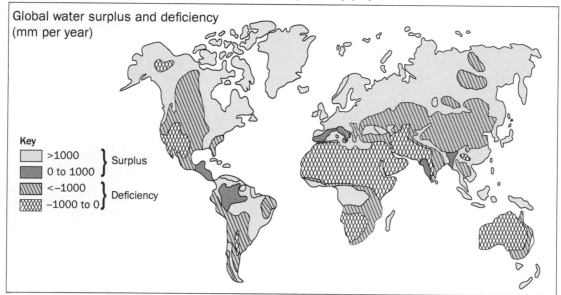

Map showing global water surplus and deficiency

In areas with a water surplus, precipitation exceeds evapotranspiration and in areas of deficit, evapotranspiration exceeds precipitation.

River basin management is all about controlling water surplus for human benefit and finding ways of creating a more reliable water supply for areas of deficit.

In the areas with a global water surplus you will find the world's largest river basins, e.g. the Amazon River. In areas of deficit higher evaporation rates may mean low precipitation is ineffective and surface rivers will only flow seasonally or not at all.

Watch this video for an explanation of global water surplus and deficit: **http://www.youtube.com/watch?v=16CeJQU1XnA**

Study the maps below as you will need to be able to interpret this range of graphical information in order to be able to describe and explain the location of river basins in different continents. In this case it is North America.

Major river basins of North America

Physical map of North America

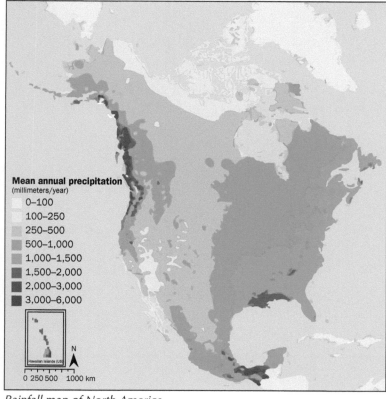

Mean annual precipitation
(millimeters/year)

- 0–100
- 100–250
- 250–500
- 500–1,000
- 1,000–1,500
- 1,500–2,000
- 2,000–3,000
- 3,000–6,000

Hawaiian Islands (US)

N

0 250 500   1000 km

Rainfall map of North America

To describe and explain the location of the river basins in North America or any other continent try to address the following points. The information below is again for North America.

General patterns of distribution and direction of flow

In North America the Great Divide is a prominent watershed running from the Bering Sea southwards along the high peaks of the Rocky Mountains into Central America. Rivers on the east of this divide flow into the Atlantic or south into the Gulf of Mexico, e.g. St Lawrence and Mississippi rivers, and those to the west, like the Colorado River, flow into the Pacific. A spur of high ground comes off the northern end of this divide and runs east-west just north of the Great Lakes and all the rivers north of this flow into the Hudson Bay and Beaufort Sea, e.g. the Nelson and the Mackenzie rivers.

The distribution of drainage basins

An explanation of the distribution of drainage basins and drainage density or the number of rivers should refer to the presence of mountain ranges as major source areas of rivers due to having greater rainfall and possibly snowmelt in spring. Drainage density in North America is greatest in the east due to the annual precipitation being over 500mm a year. Also many of these rivers are fed by snowmelt in the spring, e.g. Missouri/Mississippi in their upper basins. To the west of the 500mm isohyet annual precipitation decreases and in the south-west of the USA totals are as little as 25mm a year.

Areas of high precipitation/water surplus and areas of low precipitation and high evaporation rates

Areas east of the Great Divide have high precipitation and lower evaporation rates resulting in a water surplus. Those west of the Great Divide have the opposite.

Position of river mouths

That is, the Colorado River to the Pacific Ocean; the Hudson River to the Atlantic Ocean; and the Saskatchewan River to the Hudson Bay.

Why the world needs water management

Human demands on freshwater as a result of population increase and higher standards of living have greatly increased through time. Freshwater is vital for a large range of activities:

- Domestic use, e.g. drinking, washing
- Agriculture
- Industry
- Recreation
- Hydroelectric power

Water availability is a key factor in the development of any country. Without a reliable supply it is very difficult to improve living standards and improve the economic prospects of a country.

How can river basins be managed?

River management involves interfering with the hydrological cycle. Many rivers across the globe do not have consistent flow throughout the year and so without control and regulation cannot be a positive and reliable resource. Historical records of discharge (such as a hydrograph showing discharge over many years) can show this uneven flow.

There are a number of different ways a river system can be managed for positive social, economic and environmental benefit:

- **Building a dam and creating a reservoir**: for water storage and for controlling a river's regime to reduce the risk of flooding, e.g. the Colorado River in south-west USA and Aswan High Dam in Egypt.

- **Irrigation channels for agriculture**: since the construction of the Aswan High Dam in the Nile Valley of Egypt this fertile area can be farmed all year round, as it no longer relies on an annual flood to water the crops.

- **Transfer schemes**: moving water along aqueducts, through channels or pipes from an area of surplus to an area of deficit, e.g. from the Lake District to Manchester.

- **River diversion:** water is diverted to areas of deficit e.g. California.

The hydrograph below shows the impact of the Glen Canyon dam (built in 1963) on the discharge of the Colorado River. Once a dam has been built the hydrograph shows how the peaks and troughs in river flow have been reduced so the annual flow pattern is much more even. The advantages of this were:

- The dam reduced the size and frequency of floods.

- It reduced the amount of sediment that collected in the river, making the river therefore more efficient.

However, so that the previous river landscape and habitat are not lost altogether periodic controlled flooding is sometimes used to kick-start the natural cycle of scour (erosion) and deposition of the river channel to create new sand bars or beaches and feeding areas for fish.

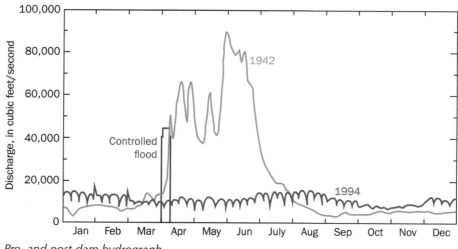

Pre- and post-dam hydrograph

Factors when considering the site of a dam

Physical	Human
Impermeable rock – so stored water does not seep away.	Low population so relocation is not too disruptive or costly.
Solid stable foundations on which the dam wall can be constructed safely.	Areas of no cultural or historical significance.
Large drainage basin with high drainage density and reliable supply of rainfall and/or snow melt.	Areas of poorer farmland where compensation to farmers is kept to a minimum.
Valley, gorge or narrow canyon – deep enough and with a small surface area (less water loss through evaporation) to store large quantities of water.	Close to agricultural areas so irrigation can be improved.
In areas not at risk of tectonic activity, i.e. unaffected by earth tremors.	Demand for electricity from hydroelectric power.

EXAM QUESTION

Discuss the physical and human factors which should be considered when selecting the site for a dam.

5 marks

Multi-purpose river basin management

These are large-scale schemes that address a number of differing demands:

- Water supply
- Regulation of river flow
- Flood control
- Hydroelectric power
- Navigation
- Recreation

Case study: The Colorado basin, USA

A multi-purpose scheme to provide a public water supply, flood control, expansion of irrigated farmland, power generation and recreation and tourism.

- Basin area: 637,137km²
- Length of Colorado River: 2,334km
- Average annual discharge: 637 m³/s
- Source: Rocky Mountains, Colorado
- Mouth: Gulf of California
- Average precipitation over basin: less than 25mm

Watch these two video clips **http://www.youtube.com/watch?v=BE1RbFJTZdI** and **http://www.youtube.com/watch?v=JAHHu6tbtow**

The Colorado River, U.S.A.

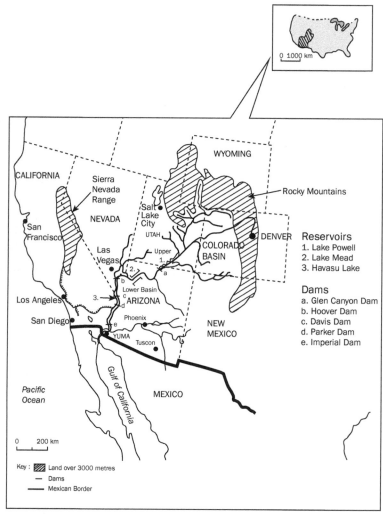

Reservoirs
1. Lake Powell
2. Lake Mead
3. Havasu Lake

Dams
a. Glen Canyon Dam
b. Hoover Dam
c. Davis Dam
d. Parker Dam
e. Imperial Dam

Key : Land over 3000 metres
— Dams
— Mexican Border

Map of the Colorado basin

Why was management needed?

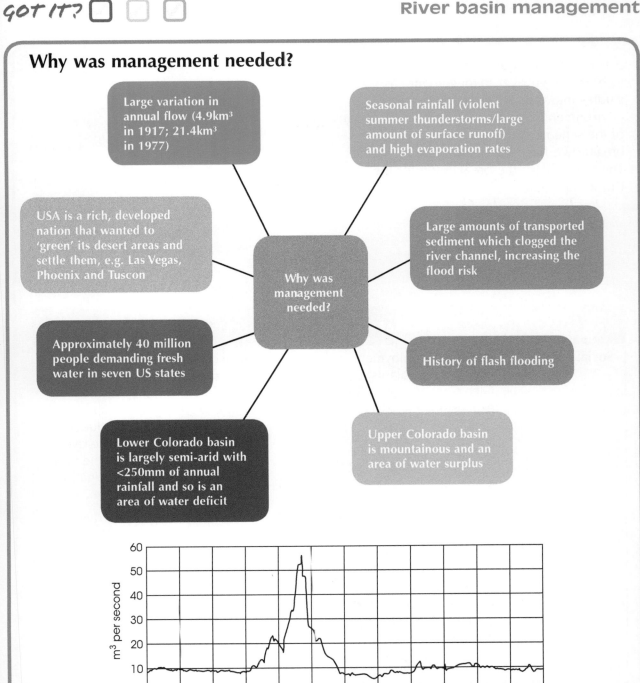

Large variation in annual flow (4.9km³ in 1917; 21.4km³ in 1977)

Seasonal rainfall (violent summer thunderstorms/large amount of surface runoff) and high evaporation rates

USA is a rich, developed nation that wanted to 'green' its desert areas and settle them, e.g. Las Vegas, Phoenix and Tuscon

Why was management needed?

Large amounts of transported sediment which clogged the river channel, increasing the flood risk

Approximately 40 million people demanding fresh water in seven US states

History of flash flooding

Lower Colorado basin is largely semi-arid with <250mm of annual rainfall and so is an area of water deficit

Upper Colorado basin is mountainous and an area of water surplus

The natural annual discharge of the Colorado

How was management imposed?

By building a series of large dams starting with the Hoover Dam in 1935 and the creation of several reservoirs, e.g. Lake Mead behind the Hoover Dam and Lake Powell behind the Glen Canyon dam.

There were political complications: the Colorado flows through seven states so the Colorado River Compact was drawn up to give each state a water allocation. This was not finalised until the mid-1960s as it was so controversial; it is still contentious today with California and Arizona being accused of exceeding their water allocation.

Any of the RBM questions will want you to break down river management case studies into the social, economic and environmental advantages and disadvantages of the scheme. You should pre-prepare this breakdown for your individual case studies. The table shows the breakdown for the Colorado River.

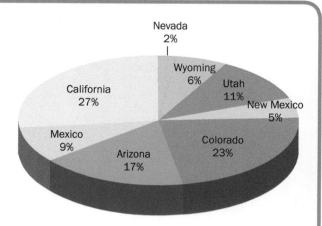

Colorado River allocation state by state

	Advantages	Disadvantages
Social	Increased employment from hydroelectric plants, e.g. Glen Canyon and industrial expansion. Increased recreation and tourism on Lake Powell, e.g. from houseboats, water skiing, kayaking. Urban water supply. Increased colonisation of the arid/semi-arid region of south-west USA. Phoenix is a boom city with some of the richest farmland in the USA due to the creation of irrigation canals.	Mexico in the Lower Colorado basin suffers by being at the end of the line with much of the Colorado having 'dried up' and prone to salinisation as, due to high evaporation rates, the river water is highly saline by the time it reaches the Mexican irrigation channels. Crops then suffer. Politics play a big part in river management in the US. Water projects can secure votes for Senators, and richer, more influential states will have more leverage when it comes to allocation. Native Indian burial grounds flooded.

	Advantages	Disadvantages
Economic	Provides a reliable water source for agricultural, industrial and public need in the south-west USA. Irrigation for farmers in the drier states of Utah, Nevada, Arizona and California. Imperial Valley in California is one of the largest irrigated areas in the world growing water-hungry lettuces and alfalfa. Large cities such as Los Angeles and San Diego demand a huge amount of water. 20 dams like the Hoover, Glen Canyon, Davis and Parker produce a large amount of electricity. The Parker Dam uses this power to pump water along the Colorado Aqueduct to farms in southern California and San Diego city. Reservoirs, e.g. Lake Powell, are a tourist attraction, offering boating and other water sports, and this generates jobs and income.	Farmers pay a very low price for their water so are very wasteful. Industry using the cheap electricity is often very polluting, e.g. steel mills in Page, Arizona.
Environmental	Flood control. More even annual discharge so less erosion. Decreased sedimentation in river channel. Reservoirs provide a habitat for wildlife and birdlife.	Destruction of wilderness areas. Trapping of silt behind the dams so sand bars and islands do not form and valuable habitats downstream disappear. Large reservoirs lose millions of cubic meters of water through evaporation every year. Loss of desert wildlife when canyons were flooded to form reservoirs.

EXAM QUESTION

Explain why there is a need for water management in a river basin you have studied.

5 marks

Development and health

In this section

- validity of development indicators
- differences in levels of development between developing countries
- a water-related disease: causes, impact, management
- primary healthcare strategies

Indicators of development

Development is the use of resources to improve the standard of living of a country. Various social and economic **indicators** are used to measure the rate and level of progress. The world's richest 1% of the population owns 50% of the world's wealth. This shows that development is uneven in the world.

TOP TIP

When referring to a developing country don't use 'Africa' as a collective for all poor countries. Africa is a continent with 54 diverse countries.

Useful terms

Rich countries	Poor countries
Developed countries	Developing countries
EMDC: economically more developed countries	ELDC: economically less developed countries
'First World'	'Third World'
e.g. UK	e.g. Tanzania

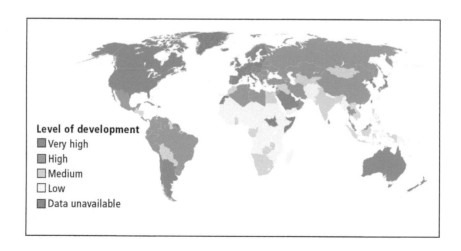

Level of development
- Very high
- High
- Medium
- Low
- Data unavailable

Relationship between social and economic indicators

Economic indicators — Standard of living	Social indicators — Quality of life
Economic indicators show how well off a country is in terms of money, the currency usually used is US$. Per capita means per person.	Social indicators show how well a country is developing in key areas such as health, education and diet.
Examples of economic indicators: • Gross National Product (GNP) per capita • Gross Domestic Product (GDP) per capita • Vehicles per thousand (‰) • Telephones ‰ • TV sets ‰ • % of people employed in agriculture • Energy consumption per capita (kw) • % of population living below the poverty line	Examples of social indicators: • Life expectancy • Birth rate • Infant mortality • Adult literacy • Number of patients per doctor • Number of calories per person per day • Gender equality • Secondary school enrolment

In most cases if a country is creating a lot of wealth (high GDP) then it will in general also have a good quality of life (long life expectancy): wealthier countries usually have healthier populations.

However some countries are an exception to this rule.

> **TOP TIP**
>
> Using the figures in the below table you could plot a scatter graph to show the relationship between wealth (GDP per capita) and health (life expectancy).

Country	GDP per capita $	Life expectancy	Adult literacy %	HDI* rank
Cuba	6051	79.4	99.8	44
India	1499	65	74.4	135
Jamaica	5290	74.8	87.9	96
Japan	38492	84.6	99	17
Tanzania	695	59	69.4	159
Turkey	10946	74.8	95.3	69
UAE	43875	79.2	77.9	40
United Kingdom	39351	79.5	99	14
Vietnam	1911	74	94	121
Source:	World Bank	WHO	UN	UN

*Human Development Index

Limitations of single indicators

The above indicators are examples of **single indicators**. They show one aspect of how the country is performing, and are very useful in giving a general idea of how the country is doing. However there are limitations to these single indicators:

- Most indicators are an average figure. For example GNP per capita is the average income of a person in a country if all of the wealth created in that country is divided equally among the population. GNP per capita does not show the inequality of wealth within a country. GNP figures are in some cases inflated by oil revenues.

- The standard of living and quality of life is generally better in the cities (because wealthy people tend to live in cities). Single indicators do not show regional variation (rural/urban), or account for other differences and inequalities, such as gender.

- Single indicators do not take into account the reasons for higher energy consumption in hot/cold countries.

- Economic indicators such as GDP/GNP/GNI per capita use US$ as a unit. This does not take into account the amount of money lost in converting a different currency into US$. It doesn't take into account the purchasing power of US$ in the local economy either, so it gives a false image of how rich/poor a country is.

- Subsistence agriculture and the information economy (bartering system) are not reflected in economic indicators.

- Some of the indicators will not apply to a country, e.g. if a country does not have widespread electricity then the number of TVs per household will be largely irrelevant.

- Data used to calculate the above single indicators will also have a degree of inaccuracy for the same reasons as inaccuracies in census data (see page 51 in the Population section).

One indicator is not enough to show how developed or underdeveloped a country is. In an attempt to have a more comprehensive indicator the United Nations uses a combined indicator called the **Human Development Index**, which is calculated by combining the adult literacy rate, life expectancy and real GNP to give a more balanced view.

TOP TIP

Learn plenty of real country examples to include in your exam answers.

Inequalities between developing countries

Out of 224 countries in the world over 100 of them are considered to be 'poor', i.e. developing countries. However, not all developing countries are equally poor.

Reasons behind global variations in development	
Physical factors:	**Human factors:**
• Climate	• Population growth
• Relief	• High levels of disease
• Resources	• Lack of industralisation and infrastructure
• Environment	• Trade/trade barriers
• Natural disasters	• Debt
• Geographical location	• Civil wars/government stability
	• Corruption
	• Education/technology

EXAM QUESTION

Referring to named developing countries that you have studied, **account for** the wide range in levels of development between developing countries.

10 marks

Malaria: water-related diseases

What is malaria?

- Malaria is an example of water-related disease found in tropical and sub-tropical areas of the world.
- About 3.3 billion people – half of the world's population – are at risk of malaria.
- In 2010, there were about 219 million malaria cases.
- Annually there are approximately 660,000 malaria deaths.
- It is an infection caused by the malaria parasite called Plasmodium.
- It is a preventable and treatable disease.

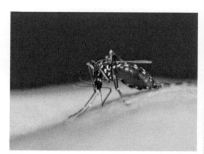

The female Anopheles mosquito is the vector/carrier of the disease

The physical and human causes of malaria

Physical	Human
Female Anopheles mosquito (vector/carrier)	High population density (blood meal)
Stagnant water – puddles, paddy fields	Shade for mosquito to rest
Moderate to high rainfall	Poor sanitation in shanty towns can contribute to areas of stagnant water
Humidity over 60%	
Altitude below 3000m (warmer)	
Temperatures 15–40°C	

Symptoms

Symptoms usually appear 9–14 days after infection and include fever, shivering, vomiting and other flu-like symptoms.

If not treated malaria can be deadly; early, accurate diagnosis (blood test) and treatment is vital.

Impact on the people and community

Malaria has serious economic impacts in Africa, slowing economic growth and development and perpetuating the vicious cycle of poverty.

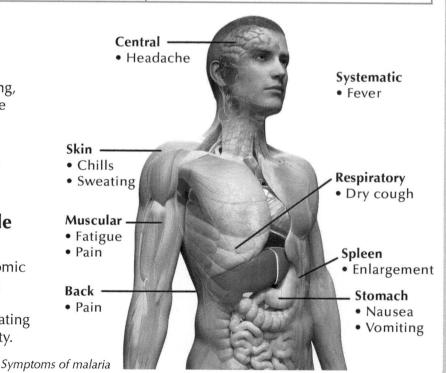

Central
- Headache

Systematic
- Fever

Skin
- Chills
- Sweating

Respiratory
- Dry cough

Muscular
- Fatigue
- Pain

Spleen
- Enlargement

Back
- Pain

Stomach
- Nausea
- Vomiting

Symptoms of malaria

Malaria is truly a disease of poverty, afflicting mainly the poor who tend to live in malaria-prone rural areas in poorly-constructed dwellings (shanty towns) that offer few, if any, barriers against mosquitos.

- Immune system can be weakened by malnutrition or other illness.
- If you are ill you are unable to work for at least 10 days, resulting in loss of income.
- Income is on average 60% lower than in non-malarial areas.
- The risk of infection is highest in the rainy season. This coincides with the agricultural peak, meaning that less food may be produced, as people cannot work.
- Chronic absenteeism in school children.
- Growth of GDP is lowered by 1–3% per year.
- Accounts for 30–50% of all hospital admissions.
- Costs up to 40% of public health expenditure.

Management

Prevention	Effectiveness
Spray insecticides – DDT	• Cheap and easy to apply but it is bad for the environment • Health risk • Banned in 2007
Spray insecticides – Malathion	• Less risky than DDT but it is expensive • It needs to be re-applied more often • Unpleasant smell
Throw mustard seeds into stagnant water – mosquito larvae get stuck to the sticky seeds and drown	• It works in small controlled areas but it is impossible to do this to all stagnant water • A waste of food
Introduce natural enemies – mosquito-eating fish like muddy loach and carp. Ducks can be released into the paddy field.	• It doesn't spoil the environment • People can eat the fish/duck – extra protein • It has been successful in parts of India and East Africa (Tanzania)
Drain breeding sites by filling depressions (holes) and planting eucalyptus trees	• Removes the breeding sites • Almost impossible to implement as the mosquito can breed in a muddy footprint • Canals need to be flushed every 5–7 days to disrupt breeding cycle – clean water is too valuable
Parasitic wasps – eat larvae	• No real danger to humans but may cause harm to the indigenous wildlife
BTI bacteria are grown on coconuts which are then thrown into stagnant water and destroy the stomach lining of larvae	• Cheap, no risk to environment • Coconuts are plentiful and often grow near stagnant water • Lasts up to 45 days • Only works in large area – not a puddle

Treatment	Effectiveness
Chloroquine	• Cheap and easy to use • Some mosquitos have developed resistance
Lariam	• Lots of side effects
Malarone	• 98% effective • Few side effects • Expensive
Quinghaosu – developed from Chinese herbal medicine (commercial name is Artemisinin)	• Fast acting • Mosquitos not becoming resistant so far • Very expensive
RTS,S – new vaccine	• Triggers the human immune system to defend the body against the malaria parasite as it enters the bloodstream • Still on trial • GlaxoSmithKline (drug company) is trying to keep the cost of this drug down
Insecticide-treated bed nets	• Lasts up to one year • Reduced incidence in Tanzania by 35%
Insect repellents and covering the skin at dawn and dusk	• Insect repellent can smell unpleasant • Covering the skin is not always practical
WHO 'Roll Back Malaria' campaign, and the Bill and Melinda Gates Foundation	• Good, but billions of dollars must be raised

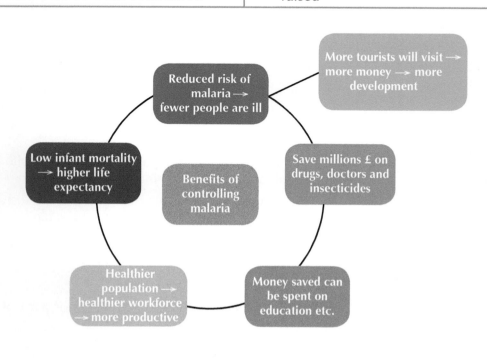

Improving health care in developing countries: 'Primary Health Care'

The World Health Organisation (WHO) was set up by the United Nations (UN) in 1948. Since then the WHO has been helping poor countries to obtain better health care. The WHO is funded by the UN.

Their main aims are to eradicate diseases with the use of:

1. Vaccination
2. Quarantine
3. Research and development into cure and prevention of infectious diseases
4. Education and better access to health care

Example of WHO's work: Primary Health Care (PHC)

Health care in many developing countries is so basic that any improvement (however small) will have a positive impact on the overall primary health care.

- Primary Health Care is the most basic level of health service.
- It's aim is to improve access to health care for EVERYONE in the country. This means providing basic health care to rural villages and settlements far into the bush lands.
- Primary health care is generally better in the city but in the slums (such as Kibera, see page 77 in the Urban section) health care and living conditions are rudimentary.

Barefoot doctors (also known as 'community health worker')

A barefoot doctor is someone in the rural village/community who received minimal basic medical and paramedical training. Their purpose is to bring health care to rural areas where urban-trained doctors would not settle.

They promote basic hygiene, preventive health care, and family planning, and treat common illnesses. They also refer patients on to a doctor and hospital if the condition is serious.

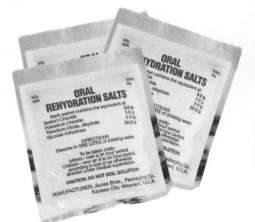

They use cheap, cost-effective treatments such as oral rehydration therapy (ORT). ORT is a cheap and effective way to treat dehydration and diarrhoea with a solution of water, salt and sugar. Diarrhoea kills about 2.2 million children every year.

Oral rehydration salts to treat dehydration and diarrhoea

Other examples of PHC

- Advice on diet and nutrition.
- Advice on food preparation.
- Family planning: giving more choice to women about reproduction and contraception.
- Basic sanitation education, e.g. washing hands and boiling water.
- Colourful information posters and wall murals about how to prevent catching diseases; they usually contain very little writing because of the high level of illiteracy in developing countries.

Health education schemes

- Linked to local schools and volunteer mothers groups – targeting suitable groups of people. Expensive but beneficial.
- Raise awareness of general health problems, the benefits of better diets and nutrition.

Mass vaccinations

- Offer protection against health problems that can kill in a developing country, such as polio, measles, whooping cough, cholera and TB.

Bamako initiative (Mali)

- 34 countries linked their hospitals, rural social services, schools, religious groups, women's and youth groups to develop PHC.
- In Benin 200 health centres were set up covering 58% of the population. Costs were spread out among local communities.
- In 1993 a vaccination programme was introduced.
- Pre- and post-natal health education set up to tackle infant mortality rates.

EXAM QUESTION

For malaria or any other water-related disease that you have studied, **discuss** the physical and human factors that put people at risk of contracting the disease.

6 marks

GOT IT? ☐ ☐ ☐

Global climate change

In this section

- physical and human causes of climate change
- local and global effects
- management strategies and their limitations

'Climate is what you expect –
weather is what you get'
Robert A. Heinlein

Causes of climate change

Physical causes of climate change

Milankovitch Cycles: global temperatures change due to the Milankovitch Cycles. These are cyclical variations in the tilt and orbit of the Earth. These alter the amount of energy the Earth receives from the sun, therefore influencing the temperature.

For more on these cycles, visit **http://channel. nationalgeographic.com/channel/videos/ ice-age-cycles/**

Sunspots: an increase in solar activity (sunspots) can lead to an increase in temperature. Solar activity tends to occur in cycles of 11 years.

Volcanic eruptions: large volcanic eruptions (e.g. Eyjafjallajökull in Iceland) can cause large quantities of ash and dust to be released into the atmosphere. This ash and dust can then absorb and scatter insolation, which lowers temperatures. If many eruptions occur in a short period of time then this can also lower world temperatures.

2002 solar activity on the left versus 2009 solar activity on the right

Changes in ocean currents: changes in deep ocean currents (e.g. the Thermohaline Current) occur in cycles of 70 years. When the currents are weaker, the climate becomes warmer.

There is a wealth of information on climate change at the BBC site here **http://www.bbc. co.uk/education/guides/z432pv4/revision/3**

Retreating/melting ice caps: melting ice caps can also reduce the Earth's albedo and consequently raise temperatures. Melting ice caps can also decrease water temperatures and salinity in the surrounding water. This can alter currents such as the North Atlantic Drift, which brings 30% of all of the heat that Western Europe receives.

Human causes of climate change

Scientists have linked climate change to an increase in the greenhouse gases in the atmosphere; although greenhouse gases are produced naturally, human activity creates much more.

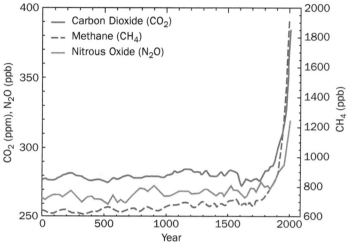

The increase in greenhouse gases in our atmosphere

Greenhouse gases contribute to global warming through the 'greenhouse effect', as shown in the figure on the right.

The main greenhouse gases are:

Carbon dioxide

- From burning fossil fuels such as coal in power stations.

- Because of deforestation (as the trees convert CO_2 to oxygen – particularly in rainforests such as the Amazon).

- From peat bog reclamation or development. Peat naturally releases CO_2, but peat bogs contain vegetation that acts as a sink for the gas. More than half of the sites for windfarms in Scotland are on highland peat, which means that the vegetation is removed and CO_2 is released.

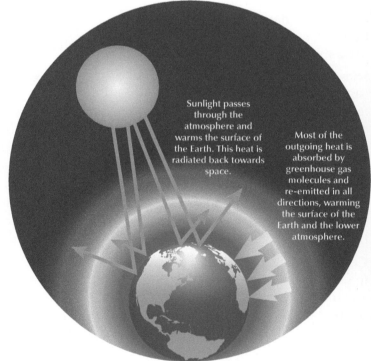

Sunlight passes through the atmosphere and warms the surface of the Earth. This heat is radiated back towards space.

Most of the outgoing heat is absorbed by greenhouse gas molecules and re-emitted in all directions, warming the surface of the Earth and the lower atmosphere.

The 'greenhouse effect'

Nitrous oxides

- These are emitted from vehicle exhausts. The number of vehicles on the road is also increasing, which in turn increases the amount of nitrous oxide being released.

Methane

- This is emitted from landfill sites, which account for almost half of the UK's methane emissions.
- An increased population leads to more food production and more rice paddies, which again emit methane.
- Methane is also produced by animals – there are more animals to accommodate for the growing population and therefore more animal dung and belching cows.

CFCs

- These are found in some aerosols, air-conditioning systems and refrigerators and can remain in the atmosphere for 400 years.

Sulphur hexafluoride

- From magnesium smelters and electrical substations.

Hydro fluorocarbons (HFCs)

- Powerful greenhouse gases used to replace CFCs in refrigeration and air-conditioning.

'Global dimming' from air pollution reduces the amount of sunlight received by the Earth. This may mean that global warming could have occurred at a level much higher than previously thought.

For more on this, read the following article:
http://www.bbc.co.uk/sn/tvradio/programmes/horizon/dimming_prog_summary.shtml

---

EXAM QUESTION

'On current climate projections, which would see global average temperatures reach about 4°C higher than pre-industrial times by 2100, a study found that 16% of species in the world would face the risk of imminent extinction purely because of climatic factors.' *Independent Newspaper*.

Both human and physical factors contribute to climate change.

Explain the physical causes of climate change.

5 marks

> ### TOP TIP
> Read the question carefully. This only asks for the physical causes.

Local impact of climate change

Glasgow City Council have stated that, 'climate change is one of the most serious challenges facing Scotland today.'

Significant trends have been identified in Scotland, for example the trends detailed below.

Average rainfall

Average rainfall has increased (there has been a 70% increase in winter precipitation in northern Scotland from 1961 to 2004), and there are more heavy rainfall events. These trends are expected to continue.

Flood defence scheme in Houston, Renfrewshire

- More flooding leads to damage to infrastructure and buildings. Salmon spawning grounds may be destroyed.

- More expensive, local flood defence schemes are needed due to increased levels of flooding.

- Traditional buildings will be wetter for longer periods of time, resulting in increased weathering of stone. This puts many of Scotland's historic buildings at risk of decay.

Maximum temperatures have increased

On average the maximum temperature has increased in Scotland by 1.21°C from 1961 to 2004.

- The length of the growing season in the west of Scotland has increased by 5 weeks since 1961; this is expected to continue and so yields will become bigger. Scotland will become more self-sufficient in terms of food supply. Diseases such as potato blight may be more difficult to control, and some non-native pests and animal diseases may become more established.

- The longer growing season will have a detrimental impact on hay fever sufferers.

- There is an increased threat of alien and non-native plant species taking over as the climate changes. The increased temperatures would prove detrimental for species such as the Arctic char.

Rising sea level of up to 2mm a year

A rise in sea level will impact on the coastlines of Scotland, destroying salt marshes and coastal settlements. Glacial isostasy (the upward movement of the Earth's crust since the end of the Ice Age) should mean that the impact in Scotland is reduced.

More heatwaves

An increase in summer heatwaves in Glasgow may eventually cause increased mortality, particularly affecting vulnerable groups in Scotland such as the elderly.

Milder winters

Milder temperatures in winter will mean even fewer snowy days in the future. There has already been a reduction in snowfall over the last century, but it is predicted that winter snowfall may reduce by 50% or more across Scotland by the 2080s. The Met Office has warned that the ski industry in Scotland could disappear within a decade.

For more on how Scotland's climate is changing, take a look at this website:
http://www.adaptationscotland.org.uk

Global impact of climate change

Climate change will have an impact on every area of the globe, however, a report from the Millennium Project states: 'Poorer countries that contribute the least to GHGs (greenhouse gases) are the most vulnerable to climate change's impacts because they depend on agriculture and fisheries, and they lack financial and technological resources to cope.'

Find out more about the Millennium Project on their website: **http://www.millennium-project.org**

Sea level rise

Sea levels are rising and are predicted to continue to rise due to melting ice caps (e.g. West Antarctic) and the warmer sea water expanding.

- Low-lying coastal areas, such as Bangladesh, will be affected most severely with large-scale displacement of people, loss of land for farming and destruction of property.
- Some islands such as the Maldives will become completely uninhabitable.
- Expensive flood protection schemes, such as the Thames Barrier, have been invested in as a result.

Extreme weather events

These will be more frequent, with hurricanes, tornadoes and storms also predicted to get stronger. This causes more damage to buildings and infrastructure and the displacement of people as they move away from hazardous areas. In some coastal locations of the USA it is almost impossible for locals to insure their homes.

Drought and flooding

Some areas will become drier; droughts will become more common in some areas, such as Ethiopia, while others become even wetter.

- In drier areas crop yields will reduce further and an increased risk of famine is possible. Mass migration will occur resulting in more environmental refugees. There is also the problem of conflict over water supplies.

Flooding in Vermont

- In wetter areas there will be an increase in flooding. Areas such as the US state of Vermont are particularly at risk.

Increase in certain diseases

- More people will be at risk from diseases such as malaria as the mosquito moves into new, more temperate areas. There will be around 40 million people exposed to the risk of contracting malaria in Africa alone.

- There will be an increase in water-borne diseases such as typhoid after floods. Developing countries will be most severely affected as their sanitation systems are not as advanced.

Ecosystems are changing and will continue to do so

- Sensitive coral and algae that live on coral are starved of oxygen, causing bleaching and the coral will eventually die out.

- Some butterflies, foxes, and alpine plants have moved farther north or to higher altitudes.

- Loss of penguins on Antarctica due to warmer conditions.

Adélie penguins on Antarctica, where their numbers have fallen from 32,000 breeding pairs to 11,000 in 30 years

EXAM QUESTION

Discuss the possible impacts of global warming throughout the world.

5 marks

Management strategies and their limitations

International strategies

Strategy	Explanation	Limitations
The **Doha Amendment** to the Kyoto Protocol	Many governments have pledged to reduce greenhouse gases by signing up to an international agreement called the Doha Amendment.	Several countries, including the USA – one of the world's biggest greenhouse gas emitters – have refused to agree to the treaty.
Development of **solar radiation management**	This is a type of geo-engineering project that aims to reduce the amount of sunlight hitting the Earth and thus tackle global warming.	This does not address the problem of more greenhouse gases in the atmosphere and other associated problems such as ocean acidification.
Development of **carbon dioxide removal**	Another type of geo-engineering project, carbon capture is the process whereby waste carbon dioxide is 'captured' and deposited where it will not enter the atmosphere.	Long-term security of underground storage is difficult to predict and there is a risk of the stores leaking back into the atmosphere.
Further development of **renewable energy sources**	Wind farms: the power of the wind is harnessed.	Some people oppose wind farms on the grounds that they are ugly, noisy and a hazard to wild birds.
	Solar energy: where sunlight is captured in solar panels and converted into electricity.	The manufacture and implementation of solar panels can be costly.
	Hydroelectric power: where the movement of water is used to generate electricity.	Dams that are constructed to produce hydroelectric power flood large areas of land. This has a huge impact on local people, wildlife, vegetation and hydrology.
	Geothermal power supply: this is possible in volcanic regions where the natural heat of the earth is used to produce steam and power turbines.	This can be expensive to construct and only works in areas of volcanic activity. Geothermal and volcanic activity may reduce, leaving power stations redundant.

Local and national strategies

Strategy	Explanation	Limitations
Afforestation	Countries reduce deforestation and increase afforestation in order to provide a 'sink' that soaks up carbon dioxide (CO_2) from the air through photosynthesis. Countries such as Bangladesh also plant trees to reduce the impact of climate change as it reduces coastal erosion.	Forests take decades to mature and so it will take some time to reap the benefits.
Carbon credits	Governments (e.g. in Australia) provide a scheme where the 'polluter pays' according to the quantity of greenhouse gases they generate.	Companies are likely to purchase carbon offsets instead of reducing emissions.
Congestion charges	In cities such as London, drivers are charged for entering the congestion charging zone. This is to discourage people from driving into the zone during peak hours and promotes the use of public transport.	Although proven very effective, this is quite unpopular and difficult to implement. Few cities have adopted this.
Targeting vehicle emissions	Governments such as here in the UK provide grants towards electric cars and tax 'gas guzzlers'. They promote small changes such as fuel efficient driving and ensuring that cars have harder tyres.	Electric cars remain expensive and do not yet offer the convenience of a diesel or petrol car.
'Reduce, reuse and recycle'	This scheme helps save energy and reduces pollution and greenhouse gas emissions from resource extraction, manufacturing, and disposal.	Overall, this has proved successful but in 2013 Scotland still only recycles 41.2% of household waste.
Promotion of energy efficient products	Lightbulbs and large electrical products in the home are now labelled to allow consumers to determine their efficiency. Government initiatives include the boiler scrappage scheme and grants for wall/loft insulation.	Effective, but the impact on overall greenhouse gas emissions is limited.

TOP TIP

Can you think of strategies in your own local area?

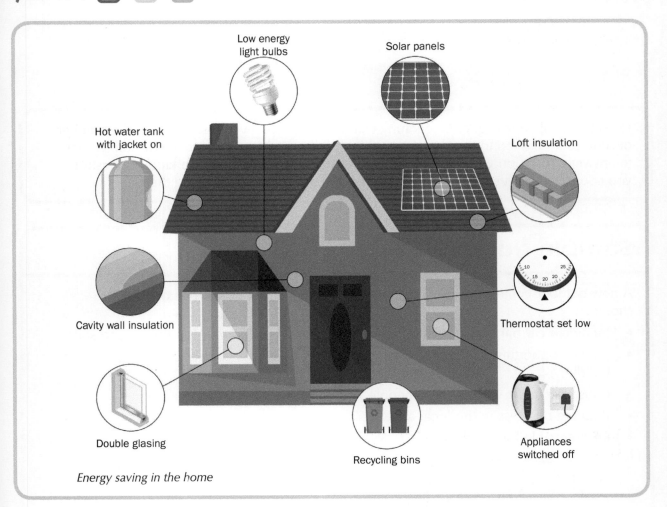

Low energy light bulbs

Solar panels

Hot water tank with jacket on

Loft insulation

Cavity wall insulation

Thermostat set low

Double glasing

Recycling bins

Appliances switched off

Energy saving in the home

Application of geographical skills question

In section 4 of your Higher Geography exam you will be given a scenario and a number of sources and asked to use the geographical skills you have developed over the course to answer a question worth 10 marks. Below are two examples of the kind of question you could find in this section, with tips on how to go about answering them.

Sample question 1

A new outdoor centre is to be constructed in grid square 8032. The outdoor centre should:

- Include a car park, main centre and overnight accommodation for visitors and staff.
- Provide opportunity for zorbing, mountain biking, assault courses, kayaking and raft building/racing.
- Cause minimum disruption to people and business in the local area.
- Promote business in the local area.
- Be accessible for coaches.

Zorbing

Using map evidence and the information from the sources below, **evaluate** the suitability of the proposed site.

10 marks

> ### TOP TIP
> With a question like this you can agree or disagree with the proposed site – as long as you explain your reasons.

Map 1

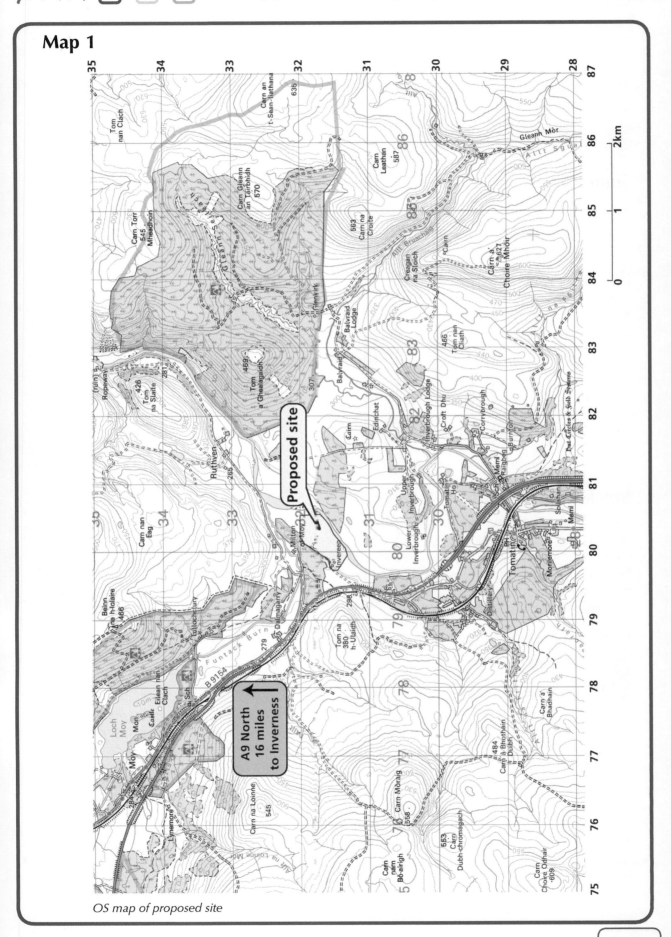

OS map of proposed site

Application of geographical skills question

Source 1

'The proposed activity centre will bring somewhere in the region of 11,000 tourists to the area each year. It will provide around 10 full time jobs and will generate around £50,000 in the local area from tourist spending.'

Local MSP

Source 2

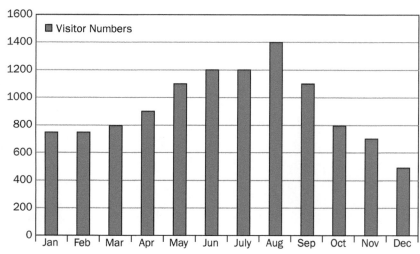

Graph showing visitor numbers

Break down the brief

Before beginning your answer, carefully study the brief and sources provided. It is helpful to use the brief when structuring your answer in separate paragraphs. This will help you develop your answer and ensure you hit all necessary points. The brief is broken down below and a sample answer is provided.

> **TOP TIP**
>
> Remember to refer to both the sources and the map. This means use grid references!

Text from the brief	Preparation/ thinking points	Example answer
1. Include a car park, main centre and overnight accommodation for visitors and staff.	• Is the land suitable for building? • What would need to be built for accommodating visitors and staff?	*The flat land at GR808320 makes it easier to build on and there is plenty of room for expansion should this be required in the future. However the land is also next to a river (Funtack Burn), which could present flooding problems.*

Text from the brief	Preparation/ thinking points	Example answer
2. Provide opportunity for zorbing, mountain biking, assault courses, kayaking and raft building/ racing.	• Think about the activities and the land they would require. • Is a large area of land needed, should it be flat or steep, etc?	*The area is located next to Funtack Burn which, if conditions permitted, would provide opportunity for some watersports including raft building and racing. The forest in 8131 could be used for the assault course as the trees could be used to provide obstacles. The steep slopes nearby at GR805328 would provide conditions for challenging walks/other sports. Kayaking could take place in the local Loch Moy in GR778340.*
3. Cause minimum disruption to people and business in the local area.	Look for local buildings and settlements on the map.	*The construction of the building and associated car park could ruin the landscape. The vehicles used for construction would be noisy and disturb local residents. The peace and tranquillity of the area could also be ruined by large groups of adults and children taking part in the outdoor activities. That said, the area is still remote and is far enough away (3km) from Tomatin to cause little disruption there.*
4. Promote business in the local area.	• What sorts of businesses would benefit? • Think about the jobs that would be created and the associated multiplier effect.	*The centre would provide 10 jobs for locals in places like Tomatin in 8028. The jobs may be more secure than the seasonal jobs offered elsewhere as visitors come to the centre all year round (as shown in the graph of visitor numbers). A lot of money (£50,000 according to the local MP) would be generated in an area with little potential for economic opportunities such as large industries. This would create the multiplier effect, allowing services in the area to further improve.*
5. Be accessible for coaches.	Look for local roads and names.	*A small road would provide access. Although this could be quite narrow, the road could be widened to accommodate coaches. It is located just off a main road (A9) providing people access from the cities and Inverness is only 16 miles away.*

Sample question 2

A well-known property developer has applied for planning permission to the city council for a residential development. Map 2 shows the proposed site shaded in purple.

The site is predominantly made up of grassed areas which slope slightly towards the south east corner. There is also a portion of 'brownfield land' upon which the former Simshill Primary School building stood.

The site is easily accessible by public transport with both King's Park and Cathcart train stations within one mile of Simshill Road. There is currently limited vehicular access to the site, however, there is potential to create a wider access route from either Simshill Road or Old Castle Road.

The site is approximately 2.39 hectares, which is about three football pitches.

Using map evidence and the information from the sources below:

(a) **Discuss** the suitability of the new housing development.

5 marks

(b) **Evaluate** the social, economic and environmental impacts of the new houses.

5 marks

> **TOP TIP**
>
> Make reference to all of the sources, including the OS map, in your discussion of the suitability of the new housing estate. You can focus on positive and/or negative factors.

Source 1

City Council's Policy on Building New Homes:

New homes should:

1. Be environmentally friendly.
2. Make use of sustainable design. For example, orientation of the land for solar panels, possibility of rainwater harvesting.
3. Provide recycling facilities.

New homes must avoid:

1. Loss of biodiversity. Must compensate for any unavoidable loss of habitat by incorporating green features such as including larger gardens and green roofs.
2. Polluting the site and the surrounding area (noise, visual, light, air).
3. Building on a flood risk area.

Source 2

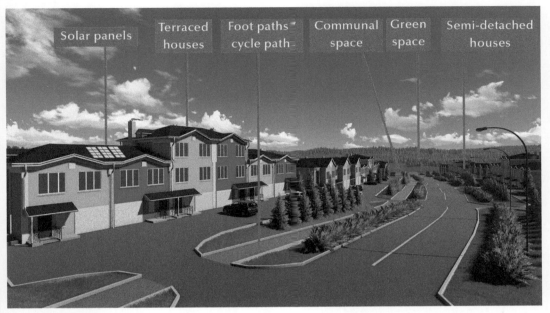

Architect's plan for the site

Source 3

Neighbourhood index 0 = poor/low 10 = excellent/high			
	Cathcart	**Glasgow average**	**Scottish average**
School attainment	9	7	8
Safety (low crime rate)	9	6	8
Average income	8	6	8
Access public transport	8	9	7
Quality of the roads	8	5	6
Air quality	9	6	8
Range of local shops	7	8	8
Range of leisure facilities	9	6	6
Access to health service	8	6	7
Employment rate	9	6	7
Total	84/100	65/100	73/100
Average property price	£255,813	£163,951	£175,627

Neighbourhood index of Cathcart, compared to Glasgow and Scottish averages

Map 1

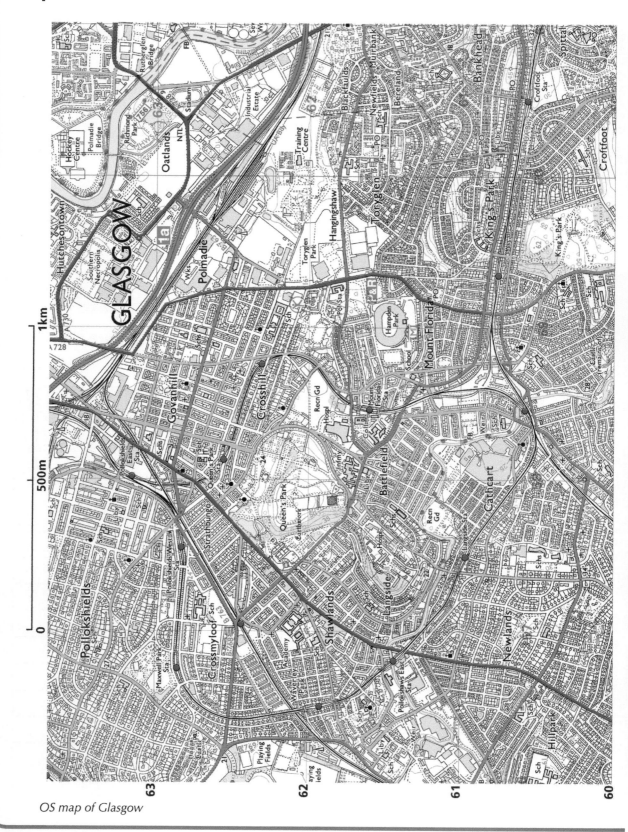

OS map of Glasgow

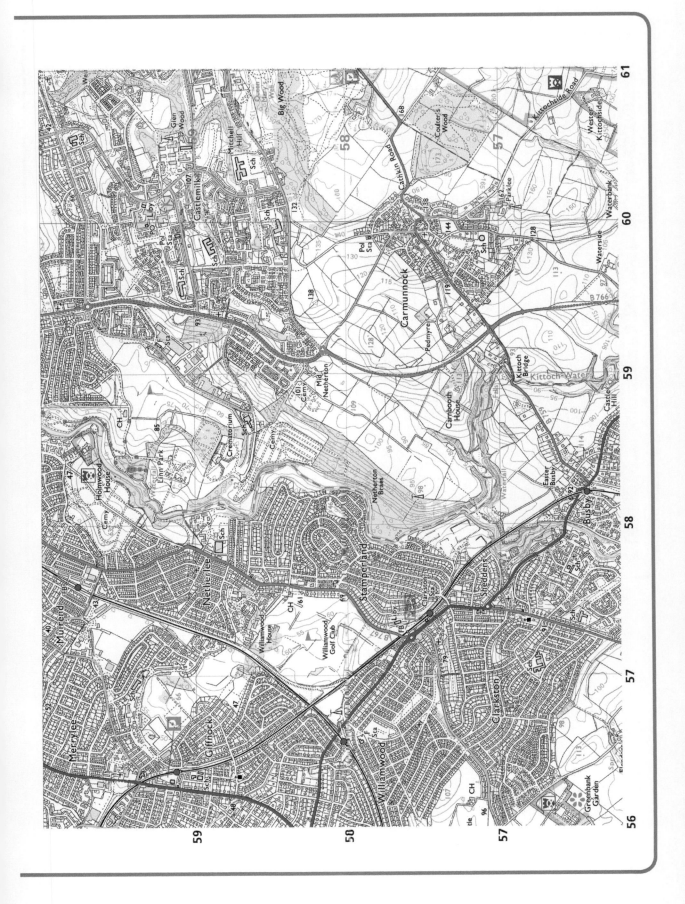

Application of geographical skills question

Map 2

Map of the proposed site

Writing your answer

Below are some points to consider when answering this question. Look at the maps and sources carefully – can you see any other important factors you should include in your answer?

Part (a)

- The proposed residential development site can be found at GR5859 on Map 1. Looking at this map it is obvious that the site isn't flat. This may add to the cost of the project as it is more difficult to build houses on a slope than on level ground.

- However, as the site is on a slope any rain water will naturally drain away to the surrounding lower ground. This may mean that a simpler and cheaper drainage system can be planned and built. It is also less likely to flood, fulfilling one of the council's specifications from Source 1.

- The site is located at the edge of the Cathcart suburb. Source 3 shows that this is an affluent neighbourhood with a high average property price and access to good schools and health services. Map 1 shows that there are at least 10 school buildings (both primary and secondary schools) close to the site.

- Maps 1 and 2 show that the site is well served by roads (many B roads which link to either the A728 or A730) and railways (Cathcart and King's Park) making commuting into Glasgow or East Kilbride easy.

- A significant area of the site is facing south or south-west which would be an ideal aspect for the installation of solar panels (as shown in Source 2). This will make the house more environmentally friendly than the older houses in the area, fulfilling one of the council's specification from Source 1.

- The site is very close to Linn Park and a golf course. It is also close to a community centre/gym in Castlemilk.

Part (b)

Socio-economic impact:

- The site isn't very big (under 3 hectares) and so it is likely that only a relatively small number of houses will be built. The local population will therefore only increase by a small amount and the current characteristics of the neighbourhood will not be changed – there should be no loss of 'community feeling'.

- The building work will provide jobs.

- Local shops and services are likely to benefit from the slight increase in population.

- The GP surgery and local schools will need to accommodate the new population, but as it is expected to be a relatively small increase this shouldn't stretch the local services.

- Someone in the local area may object to the planning permission no matter how 'good' the plan, and this may create tension in the local community.

Environmental impact:

- As this site is a former primary school ('brownfield' site) there isn't going to be a great loss of biodiversity or loss of habitat for the local wildlife, fulfilling one of the council's specifications from Source 1.

- The local area may experience a slight rise in noise pollution during the rush hour due to increased numbers of cars in the areas, which is contrary to one of the council's specifications from Source 1.

Glossary

Albedo: The proportion of the incident light or radiation that is reflected by a surface. Forests have a low albedo, whereas ice has a high albedo.

Atmosphere: The layer of gases that surround the Earth consisting mainly of Nitrogen and Oxygen.

Attrition: Rock fragments (stones and pebbles) hit against each other and so are reduced in size.

Biodiversity: The variety of plant and animal life in the world or in a particular habitat.

Blow hole: These are formed as sea caves grow landwards and upwards into vertical shafts and expose themselves towards the surface.

Census: Population count and survey which is carried out every 10 years in most countries.

Cirrus: Thin, wispy clouds.

Cloud seeding: The scientific process of increasing a cloud's potential to produce precipitation.

Coriolis effect: The anticlockwise rotation of the Earth deflects winds to the right in the northern hemisphere and to the left in the southern hemisphere.

Counter-urbanisation: When people move out of the city and inner city to live in the countryside.

Cumulonimbus: A dense, towering, vertical cloud associated with thunderstorms and atmospheric instability.

Deficit: Not enough.

Demographic: Study of population.

Dendro-chronology: The scientific method of dating based on the analysis of patterns of tree rings.

Differential erosion: When different materials erode at different speeds. This is due to one being more resistant than the other.

Emigration: When people move away from one country.

Evapotranspiration: The combined loss of land and water surfaces and from plants through pores (stomata) in their leaves.

Fjord: A U-shaped valley which is drowned by the sea, producing a long sea inlet.

Forced migration: The movement of people from their country of origin to another in search for safety from war, environmental disaster or religious or ethnic persecution.

Geothermal energy: Thermal energy generated and stored in the Earth.

Glacial isostasy: The rise of land masses that were depressed by the huge weight of ice sheets during the last glacial period.

Glacier: A slow moving mass of ice.

Greenhouse gases: A gas in an atmosphere that absorbs and emits radiation and therefore contributes to global warming. These gases include carbon dioxide and methane.

Groundwater abstraction: The use of water from underlying rock layers.

Gyre: The ring-like system of ocean currents rotating clockwise in the northern hemisphere and anticlockwise in the southern hemisphere.

Harmattan: A very dry, dusty easterly or north-easterly wind on the West African coast, occurring from December to February.

Human Development Index: A measure developed by the United Nations Development Programme which ranks national development based life expectancy, educational attainment, and per capita income.

Hydraulic action: When water, under great pressure, gets into cracks in rock and the pressure squeezes the air, loosening pieces of rock.

Immigrant: A term given to a person who has recent arrived in a new country.

Immigration: When people move into another country.

Insolation: This is the total amount of solar radiation energy received on a given surface area during a given time.

Irrigation: The artificial application of water to farmland.

Isohyets: A line on a map connecting points having the same amount of rainfall in a given period.

Long-term migration: When people decide settle somewhere else permanently.

Mega city: An urban settlement with population of more than 10 million.

Migration: The movement of people from one place to another. Movement from within a country is called internal migration, and between two different countries it is called international migration.

Milankovitch Cycles: The collective changes in the Earth's movements and effect upon its climate. It is named after the Serbian geophysicist and astronomer Milutin Milanković.

Ocean acidification: The ongoing decrease in ocean pH caused by human CO_2 emissions, such as the burning of fossil fuels.

Paeleo-indicators: 'Ancient' indicators which can be used to work out what the climate used to be like, for example ice cores and coral.

Refugee: Term given to people who flee their home country in search of safety.

Roche Moutonnee: An area of resistant rock which the ice has passed over. They are smooth and gently sloping on one side, and are jagged on the area facing downhill.

Rural–urban migration: When people leave their homes in the countryside in search for education or employment in the city.

Short-term migration: Seasonal migration of agricultural workers or international students studying abroad for their degrees, for example.

Subsistence farming: When farmers grow crops and rear animals to feed just themselves and their family, and not to sell.

Sunspots: A temporary phenomena on the sun whereby dark spots appear and extra energy is released.

Surplus: Too much or extra.

Truncated spurs: Before glaciations, valleys are made up of interlocking spurs which rivers meander around and form. The glacier effectively cuts them off creating cliff-like truncated spurs.

Urban sprawl: When towns and cities grow out into the countryside.

Urbanisation: The growth of towns and cities.

Urban–rural migration: When people leave their city lives in search of a quieter life in the countryside.

Voluntary migration: The movement of people from one place to another based on family links or economic prospects.

Westerlies: The belt of prevailing westerly winds in medium latitudes in the southern hemisphere.

Specimen answers for sample exam questions

Atmosphere

Sample exam question 1 (page 5)

At the poles (X), the sun's rays are more spread out over a larger surface area. This is because the rays strike at an angle. In comparison, at the tropics (Y) the rays are more concentrated over a smaller surface area. This is because the rays strike vertically, which means that more energy is received at the tropics. There is more atmosphere for the rays to travel through at the poles (A) than there is at the tropics (B). This means more insolation is reflected and absorbed before reaching the poles and therefore less energy is received at the poles. The Equator receives around 12 hours of daylight each day throughout the year. However, as the earth is tilted on its axis, the poles receive less daylight. For example, the North Pole is dark continuously for 6 months. More insolation is absorbed as the tropics have more vegetation, which has a lower albedo. More insolation is reflected at the poles as they have more icy surfaces, which have a higher albedo.

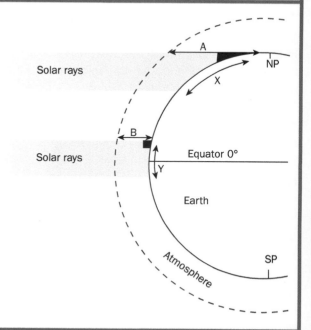

Sample exam question 2 (page 8)

Warm water in the Gulf of Mexico expands and spreads out, moving north towards the poles. This current is known as the Gulf Stream. The Coriolis effect deflects this current to the right. As the Gulf Stream reaches Europe, some of it is deflected southwards and becomes the cold Canary Current, where it returns to the Gulf of Mexico. This completes one loop, known as a gyre. The remaining warm water is deflected north as the North Atlantic Drift. As it passes Norway, the North Atlantic Drift meets north-easterly winds and so is dragged southwards. The cold water at the poles sinks and moves south as the East Greenland Current and the Labrador Current. These currents move south to join the Gulf Stream, completing another gyre. The ocean currents in the North Atlantic form a 'figure of 8' pattern.

Hydrosphere

Sample exam question 1 (page 14)

The drainage basin is an open system, with inputs, outputs, stores and transfers. Solar energy powers the processes within the drainage basin system and might be considered the main input; the other input into this system is precipitation. Water is transferred around the system by surface runoff when the rainfall falls onto an impermeable surface. If the rock is permeable the rainfall will percolate through the pores in the rock, or it might be infiltrated into the soil. It will then move downwards until it reaches the water table. From there it will move through the ground as throughflow, where it will eventually flow into the river. When the precipitation falls onto plants, it is intercepted and flows down the trunk of the plant as stem flow, where again it will meet the water table. The main outputs in a drainage basin system are evaporation from rivers and lakes as well as transpiration from plants and other vegetation. Water will also be lost from the system when the river flows into the sea. There are many places where water can be stored in the system, which may be on the surface or underground. The main surface storage includes rivers, lakes, glaciers and vegetation, while underground storage includes groundwater and soil storage.

Sample exam question 2 (page 18)

Rainfall began at 05.00 on the 26th July. It reached a peak at 08.00 when 6.25mm of rain fell. The river levels remained steady until 03.00 where they began rising slowly, possibly due to an earlier period of rain. A more rapid increase in discharge occurred at 11.00 when the rising limb increased from 0.5m to a peak of 0.7m at 18.00. The lag time therefore was 10 hours. The longer lag time may be due to flat or gently sloping land meaning it takes longer for the rainfall to reach the river. There may also be a lot of soil cover and vegetation in the area, which infiltrates and intercepts the rainfall into the soil, making it take much longer to reach the river channel. It might be quite a large drainage basin, which will take longer for the rainfall to reach the river. From 14.00 to the end of the graph, the river levels continue to drop to 0.5m at 24.00.

Lithosphere

Sample exam question 1 (page 28)

An arête forms when snow collects in two hollows back-to-back. The snow then compresses, turning to firn/neve, then ice. Due to gravity, this ice moves downhill as a glacier. Freeze-thaw weathering erodes the back of the hollow. This is when meltwater enters cracks in the rock, freezes and expands by 9%. This forces the crack wider and, when this process is repeated many times, the rock will break apart. Plucking – when the glacier freezes onto the rock and tears away the loose rock – occurs as it moves down the mountainside and this makes the back wall much steeper. The base of the hollow becomes deeper through abrasion – where pieces of rock, embedded in the bottom of the glacier, scrape and wear down the rock underneath as the glacier moves. After the ice melts two armchair shaped hollows, or corries, are left in the mountainside. The knife-edged ridge in between the corries is an arête and an example is Striding Edge in the Lake District.

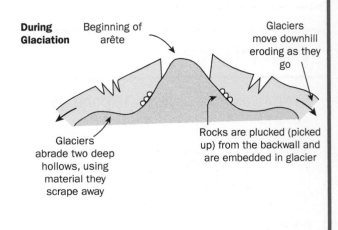

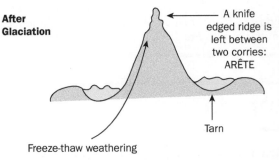

TOP TIP

Remember to include examples

Sample exam question 2 (page 42)

Dorset Coast

Around 90% of people arrive by car or coach to the Dorset Coast. The access roads are quite often narrow and therefore cannot deal with the large volume of traffic. Furthermore, there is a lack of appropriate parking and many cars park illegally on the heath land and roadsides. This slows the traffic down as vehicles try to

Answers to questions

pass parked cars on single lane roads and this can inconvenience residents. Vehicles also cause noise pollution that disrupts the peace of the local area. The car exhausts emit nitrous oxides which cause air pollution linked to various cancers and poor health.

The South West Coastal Path is used by 200,000 people each year. Many people wander off from the footpaths and destroy the heath land, while others walk at the edges and widen the path. This can scar the landscape, ruining the views. Heavy jeeps are sometimes used on the sand dunes for recreational driving. This destroys the fragile grasses that can then cause dunes to be destabilised.

The loud noises created by various activities such as jet skiing can disturb and scare off birds, and many bird watchers visit the area. Loud noises can also scare fish, which means fishermen are often in conflict with those who participate in noisy water sports. Yachts in the bay can cause water pollution and this affects those wanting to swim in the area.

Like in many other busy areas, litter remains a problem, as tourists do not always bin their rubbish. Dog fouling is a further problem on beaches, e.g. Studland Heath. If an area becomes littered, then people are less likely to visit, reducing tourist revenue.

Many of the jobs at the Dorset Coast are seasonal (mainly only for the summer months), which means that there can be high unemployment during winter months. Many houses and other types of accommodation have become second homes, bought by wealthy people from the cities, and these can lie empty for a large part of the season. This causes house prices to inflate and locals are then forced out, as they cannot afford the costs. Various local services such as primary schools then close as those who own the second homes do not need to use these services.

Biosphere

Sample exam question 1 (page 49)

Podzol soils form in cool, wet climates where precipitation exceeds evaporation. The wet climate leads to leaching and podzolisation, which cause an impermeable iron pan to form in between the A and B horizons. Leaching and podzolisation is when iron and aluminium oxides are removed from the A horizon to the B horizon. The cold climate means that decomposition is very slow and therefore there is only a very thin layer of humus in a podzol soil. Podzol soils are found under coniferous forests. This creates acidic or mor conditions in the soil. Coniferous trees do not shed their leaves every year and therefore there is only a small amount of litter; also pine needles do not decompose very quickly. There are very few soil biota found in podzol soils due to the acidic conditions and because of the cold climate. This means that podzol soils have very distinct layers. Podzol soils are found in high areas. The formation of the iron pan between the A and B horizons means that the A horizon is often waterlogged as precipitation cannot permeate through the iron pan; this can lead to gleying in the A horizon.

Population

Sample exam question 1 (page 55)

In some ELDCs there are a large number of tribal people who migrate in search of better pasture, better farming ground or better opportunities. There are also indigenous people in remote corners of the Brazilian rainforest; these people may be missed out on the census or, due to their mobile nature, counted twice. Countries like South Africa and Kenya have large urban populations who live in shanty towns and in other informal settlements. People living in such accommodation will be difficult to count because they do not have proper addresses to which the census forms may be sent out, or for the enumerator to visit. Countries such as Sudan and DR Congo have vast territories to cover with some challenging terrains. In addition Sudan and DR Congo also suffer from poor communication and crumbling infrastructure, which make it extremely difficult to reach everyone, and those living in remote villages are often unaccounted for. In Papua New Guinea over 800 languages are spoken; other countries like Nigeria (500) and India (427) also have the same problem of needing to translate the census into the vast numbers of languages and dialects. It is impossible to accurately translate every word in every question and it is also very difficult to collate all the information onto one useable database. The considerable costs involved in printing, training enumerators, distributing forms and analysing the results can make conducting a census impossible, especially when the country may have more pressing problems like housing and education. In Burkina Faso 80% of the population is illiterate, which means people require enumerators to complete the census, and this could lead to errors and omission. People may be suspicious and unwilling to give private information to an enumerator and may provide false information. Countries that recently suffered civil war (Syria) and ethnic tension (Rwanda) may find it very difficult to collect certain information such as religion and ethnic group, as people may be afraid of prosecution.

Sample exam question 2 (page 65)

Donor country, e.g. Poland

Advantages

Large numbers of young families have left Poland so pressure on local services such as education, healthcare and housing is reduced. The main demographic who immigrate are the working-age population, therefore pressure on jobs is reduced and levels of unemployment will fall. As young working-age people move away the birth rate is lowered so population growth rates will slow. Money sent home by the migrants will boost the local economy and migrants will learn new skills and may then return with these skills to their home country.

Disadvantages

The active and most educated people leave, known as the 'brain drain', resulting in a skills shortage in donor countries. Poland is experiencing a skills shortage in jobs related to building and the service industry. Families are divided and death rates may increase due to the ageing population. Family members remaining in the country of origin may become dependent on remittances being sent home by migrant workers.

Recipient country, e.g. Scotland

Advantages

The short-term gap in labour is filled. Many migrants are highly skilled, e.g. engineers and academics. Migrants will take jobs that locals did not want and will work for lower, more competitive wages, thus reducing labour costs. Migrants will enrich the culture of the area that they move to with language (according to the 2011 Census 1% of the UK's population speak Polish – which means Polish is the most commonly spoken language after English), food and music – for example most supermarkets now sell Polish groceries. The increased population will result in an increase in the tax paid to the government, which can be invested in improving local services.

Disadvantages

Migrant workers may feel discriminated against due to feelings of resentment created by fewer jobs being available, this in turn may raise unemployment figures for the local population. Ghettos/slums may develop in parts of cities and there may be a shortage of affordable housing, for example Govanhill in Glasgow. The cost of providing services for the migrant population and their families will increase, e.g. for schooling, healthcare, etc.

Rural

Sample exam question 1 (page 71)

a) Stone bunds or lines are placed across the slope parallel with the contours to reduce surface runoff. These lines dam the rainfall giving it time to infiltrate. The lines can take up some of the available crop land, but they have been shown to increase yields and reduce soil erosion. They are very cost effective as no special equipment or materials are needed, and the building of the lines can be done by members of the community. In Mali and Burkina Faso this method has been successful and some crop yields have increased by as much as 50%.

b) Another strategy that has been effective in the Tigray region of Ethiopia is keeping grazing animals, particularly goats that eat all types of vegetation cover, in an enclosed area rather than letting them wander over the landscape. This means overgrazed ground is kept to a minimum and vegetation cover in other

Answers to questions

areas remains or has a chance to re-establish itself leading to a reduction in surface runoff and soil erosion. The animals' feed is supplemented with other fodder that is grown elsewhere. However, fencing can be too expensive for the farmers, or may not be available. In some areas (such as Korr in Northern Kenya) whole woodland areas have been destroyed by farmers harvesting material to construct livestock enclosures, these woodlands may have previously been a source of food for the animals. In addition to this, all the farmers in the area may not agree on the need for fencing which could cause tensions and also make the strategy less effective if some animals in the area were still free to roam.

Sample exam question 2 (page 71)

As crops fail, families turn to 'famine foods', e.g. leaves, to supplement their diets. Such foods are nutritionally poor, the population's health will suffer and people may starve to death. Rural–urban migration increases as people are 'pushed' to leave the countryside for the cities in search of food and work, and here they will often end up living in informal settlements (shanty towns) on the edge of urban areas. This migration threatens the traditional nomadic way of life and leads to a demographical imbalance as people leave the area. As food and water become scarce, different tribal groups may be forced to live closer together near sources of water, and this can cause ethnic tensions. It can also lead to over-cultivation of that land as people are forced to farm much closer to one another. As income falls education levels will likely also fall as fewer people with the skills to teach will be left in the area, and the loss of income will mean many families will not be able to afford schooling for their children in any case. International aid is often necessary to ensure the survival of communities, but this can lead to an over-dependence on aid.

Urban

Sample exam question 1 (page 77)

Glasgow

In order to improve the flow of traffic in the city centre, Glasgow city council have introduced one-way systems: St Vincent Street and Hope Street are examples. This solution has somewhat improved the flow of traffic, however it can be frustrating to drivers who need to drive the 'long way' in order to get to their destination. Drivers who are not used to the one-way system can also find it confusing and therefore drive more slowly, which could cause traffic congestion.

Traffic wardens patrol the streets of the central business district (CBD) in order to discourage drivers from parking illegally. Drivers are fined if they disobey the parking rules, which generates funds for the city council. The council have also made street parking more expensive in order to discourage people. In recent years a few multi-storey car parks have been built in and around the city. These car parks are well used, especially during the weekend, and this has reduced the amount of cars parked on the street.

Glasgow city council with joint funding from the Scottish Government and the European Union have made improvements to old roads, built new ones (bypass) and extended the M74 motorway. Building new infrastructure will help to reduce traffic. However, increased accessibility may encourage more people to drive, so it can also lead to more cars on the road. New road bridges (Millennium Bridge) and footbridges (Tradeston (known as the 'squiggly' bridge) have been built in recent years to ease the flow of traffic and encourage people to walk to work.

In order to encourage more people to use the public transport system, many improvements have been made. New trains and buses with Wi-Fi have been very popular with commuters. Train and subway stations have been renovated. There are plans to renovate Queen Street Station in Glasgow.

Designated bus lanes throughout the city have improved the flow of traffic. These lanes can only be used by buses, taxis and bicycles; this is an inconvenience to a car user but may encourage more people to take the bus or cycle to work.

There are three Park and Ride subway stations close to Glasgow. This scheme allows drivers to park at the subway station car park at a reduced rate. Subway stations such as Shields Road have the capacity to park 800 cars.

Some firms and companies located in the city have introduced 'flexi-time' – this means commuters do not need to all rush into the city at the same time, but can stagger their arrival and departure time.

Sample exam question 2 (page 79)

Kibera, Kenya

The population of Kenya's largest slum is growing at 5% annually; this means overcrowding is a major problem. The extremely high population density creates many problems as already over-stretched resources such as water and electricity have to be shared more widely, creating tensions within the slum community. The combination of poor nutrition and lack of sanitation accounts for many illnesses and high death rates, leading to higher infant mortality rates and lower life expectancy.

In Kibera the majority of the population rent their accommodation from private landlords. The rental market isn't regulated and is mostly untaxed by the central government. Private landlords are not obliged to invest money in order to improve the standard of accommodation, therefore people rent small, substandard shacks, without running water or electricity. Family members and often extended family members share the small space. Due to lack of money the majority of the dwellings are built using cheap and unsuitable building materials, often with no proper ventilation in the kitchen.

Unemployment and underemployment is high in Kibera. Many work in the informal sector doing manual and unskilled jobs, which are often poorly paid. These jobs are also not taxed so the Kenyan government cannot raise tax revenue from the economic activities in the slum. Due to the poor living conditions, lack of jobs and chronic poverty, the area suffers from drug and alcohol abuse and a high crime rate.

The environment quality of Kibera is very poor. Due to the high population density and use of firewood and kerosene for cooking and lighting, the air quality is poor. In addition the area suffers from rush hour traffic congestion. There are some organised refuse and recycling collections but not enough to clear the rubbish created by one million people, and as a result the streets and rivers are covered with rubbish. Water quality is also very poor due to constant contamination by sewage and other human waste.

River basin management

Sample exam question 1 (page 85)

Physical factors

The dam should be built at a point where there is hard, impermeable rock such as granite as this will ensure that water does not seep away into the rock. There need to be solid and stable foundations on which the dam wall can be safely constructed. There should be a large, deep valley behind the dam so that a large volume of water can be stored. It should be built at a narrow point in the valley to reduce the length of the dam and therefore the building costs. The area should not be at risk of earthquakes to ensure the dam is not damaged by tremors. The drainage basin should be large with a high drainage density and reliable precipitation or supply of snowmelt.

Human factors

The area should have a low population to avoid the displacement of people and businesses and to keep relocation costs low. If possible the area should be poor farmland to keep compensation payments to farmers low and avoid destroying valuable, fertile lands. It should not be built in areas of historical, environmental or cultural significance as this could lead to political tensions and costly legal action. There should be demand for water nearby, for example it could be close to agricultural areas so irrigation and power created by a hydroelectric dam could be utilised.

Sample exam question 2 (page 89)

The Colorado in North America

There are forty million people in seven US States living within the Colorado basin, all needing fresh water. The Colorado River had to be managed because its annual flow was very unpredictable; annual rainfall in this part of USA is very seasonal and in places very low due to the arid/semi-arid climate (there is less than 250mm of rain annually in the lower basin). However, during the summer months (July/August) violent thunderstorms resulted in flash floods, and a lack of infiltration led to large amounts of surface runoff causing soil erosion. There were also large amounts of transported sediment which clogged the river channel, increasing the risk of flood. The lower Colorado basin has a large and growing population, all demanding water for domestic use, farming, recreation, hydroelectric power etc., yet it had a water deficit, whereas the mountainous Upper Colorado basin had a water surplus – this needed to be balanced. In addition to this, the USA is a rich and developed nation and wanted to 'green' its desert areas and allow people to settle there – cities of this kind including Las Vegas, Phoenix and Tucson are among the fastest growing cities in the USA.

Development and health

Sample exam question 1 (page 93)

Natural resources/minerals

Oil-rich countries like Saudi Arabia can earn lots of money from selling their oil. Other countries (Brazil, Ecuador) that have lots of mineral reserves will benefit in the same way.

If foreign companies obtain rights to drill and mine for minerals in these places the government (Brazil, Ecuador) can charge various taxes that will benefit these developing countries. Wealth created by natural resources eventually trickles down to the rest of the population.

On the other hand, countries like Ethiopia have very few natural resources that are in demand so these countries (also e.g. Somalia, Eritrea) attract very little foreign investment and therefore remain underdeveloped.

Political stability

Countries like Sudan/South Sudan and Syria have unstable government. This means these countries are in the middle of a civil war or a revolution.

In such places people are spending all their energy fighting and surviving. Three years of unrest in Syria has set the country back around 35 years (e.g. roads, factories, farms and buildings destroyed).

Countries experiencing civil war will not attract foreign investment as it is too dangerous. On the other hand countries like India, South Africa and Ghana have good stable government within working democracies. If these places also have natural resources they are considered to be a great development opportunity.

Strategic locations

Some countries are landlocked and this makes it difficult to trade with other countries. Some countries may also have poor infrastructure and communication so they remain set apart and remote from development (e.g. Afghanistan).

Other countries may be located next to a volatile country that suffers the consequence of poor security (e.g. Northern Pakistan and terrorist attacks).

Countries like Malaysia and South Korea are well located to trade with a wide range of countries. They also benefit from investment from countries like the USA, which continues to have a geo-political interest in the region.

Government attracting foreign companies

Countries like Thailand, Vietnam, South Korea (most Southeast Asia and far Asian countries) have invested a lot of money into educating their population (highly skilled/English speaking) so that they can attract foreign companies to set up their factories.

These countries also offer other incentives (reduced tax, free factory rent sites) to attract investors.

Natural disasters

Bangladesh and Philippines – flood.

Central America – hurricane.

Countries that suffer from natural hazards take a long time to recover and rebuild. This makes them a risky investment and so fewer foreign companies will take the risk.

<u>Tourism</u>

Countries like Brazil (2014 football World Cup, 2016 Olympics) benefit from increased tourism. Growth of tourism brings in jobs that in turn bring valuable foreign currencies ($, £), which in turn improve the living standard of people in Brazil.

Other countries that also benefit from growth in tourism include Morocco and Malaysia.

<u>Corruption</u>

Countries like Zimbabwe and Kenya are underdeveloped due to problems related to corruption. Not all money earmarked for development gets used for that purpose. Some of the money ends up in offshore bank accounts of corrupt government officials. Zimbabwe suffers from hyper-inflation, i.e. the Zimbabwe $ is worth next to nothing on the currency market.

Sample exam question 2 (page 98)
<u>Malaria</u>

<u>Physical Factors:</u>

Malaria is caused by a parasite spread by a vector, the female Anopheles mosquito. Mosquitos thrive in a warm (15–40°C) and humid (60% humidity) environment, therefore they are found in tropical coastal areas. Mosquitos need to be close to stagnant water (puddles, paddy fields) in order to reproduce. Mosquitos are most active at night, as they don't like to be in the sunlight, so during the day they need shady places to rest.

<u>Human Factors:</u>

Female Anopheles mosquitos need to drink blood to reproduce so it is ideal to be close to a densely populated area, like a shanty town (blood reservoir). People who live and work close to paddy fields are often bitten. In a developing country lots of communities do not have running water so people go to the local river to collect water; this makes people easier targets for the mosquitos. Houses in shanty towns are poorly built with inadequate windows and doors; this means mosquitos can get into the house easily and bite people in their sleep. Due to lack of knowledge and education, people living in malaria-risk areas may not sleep under a mosquito net, and their exposed skin while sleeping is ideal for the mosquito to bite.

Global climate change

Sample exam question 1 (page 101)
One reason global temperatures change is due to the Milankovitch Cycles. These are cyclical variations in the tilt and orbit of the Earth. These alter the amount of energy the Earth receives from the sun, therefore influencing the temperature. More solar activity (sunspots) can lead to an increase in temperature. For example, when there is a large amount of solar activity, then temperatures tend to rise and this usually happens every 11 years. Large volcanic eruptions (e.g. Eyjafjallajökull in Iceland) can cause massive quantities of ash and dust to be released into the atmosphere. This ash and dust can then absorb and scatter insolation, which lowers temperatures. If many eruptions occur in a short period of time then this can also lower world temperatures. The changes in deep ocean currents (the Thermohaline Current) can also cause temperatures to fluctuate. When the currents are weaker, the climate becomes warmer. Melting ice caps can also reduce the Earth's albedo and consequently raise temperatures. Melting ice caps can also decrease water temperatures and salinity in the surrounding water. This can alter currents such as the North Atlantic Drift, which brings 30% of all of the heat that Western Europe receives. Local wind patterns such as El Niño can also cause temperatures to rise and fall below seasonal averages.

Sample exam question 2 (page 104)
One impact of global warming is a rise in sea level. This occurs as the water gets warmer and expands, and also by the melting of glaciers and ice caps. Low-lying coastal areas, Bangladesh for example, will therefore be affected by the rising water. There will be large-scale displacement of people and a loss of

Answers to questions

farmland. Across the globe there will also be more extreme and more variable weather, including floods, droughts, hurricanes and tornadoes. There will also be an increase in precipitation, particularly in the winter in northern countries such as Scotland. This will increase flooding in these areas, which will lead to costly repairs and prevention methods. Some areas, like the Great Plains in the USA, may experience drier conditions. This will mean more irrigation will need to take place (which is expensive) and crop yields may reduce. There will be an increase in the extent of tropical diseases as areas get warmer – roughly 40 million more people in Africa will be at risk of contracting malaria. This will hinder development further in different areas. There will be longer growing seasons in many areas of northern Europe, increasing food production and a range of crops being grown. Moreover, wildlife will be affected. It is predicted that there will be the extinction of at least 10% of land species as they will not be able to acclimatise quickly enough. There will be changes to ocean current circulation, for example in the Atlantic, as the thermohaline circulation will start to lose its impact on north-western Europe, resulting in considerably colder winters.